## Shopping & Leisure Guide to
# Lille

© 2004 by Passport Guide Publications
19 Morley Crescent, Edgware
Middlesex HA8 8XE

| | |
|---|---|
| Written By: | Sharron Livingston |
| Published By: | Passport Guide Publications |
| Enquiries : | Tel: 020 8905 4851 |
| Email: | Sharron@channelhoppers.net |
| Web site: | www.channelhoppers.net |

ISBN: 1-903390-03-6

# Contents

# Contents

# Introduction

**Lille is the Capital of Flanders
A City for the Young and the Young at Heart!**

Just 20 years ago, Lille was a sad, run-down town with an ailing textile industry.

Since then local business has taken the town in hand and Lille has renovated itself to the point of chic, got itself onto the Eurostar train route and has filled its streets with designer shops, boutiques and countless gastronomic restaurants.
And all of this is packaged in a town of cobbled streets, quaint architecture and beautiful buildings.

What's more, no less than five motorways converge there, it has its own airport and the high speed TGV train gets there in just 2 hours from London. The message is clear: 'welcome'.

In fact, tourists are so welcome that local retailers have developed a 'help-the-tourist' programme. A group of helpers called 'The Stewards' dress in bright yellow jackets and patrol the busy areas in search of tourists in need. They answer questions, give directions, give out free maps of the city, and generally act as friendly guides.

Lille is especially rife with retail activity, from street peanut vendors, to the colourful markets and the spectacular range of designer wear from factory shopping and discounted haut couture, all of which are highlighted within these pages.

In one small region you have a mix of Flemish and European style, culture and cuisine, historical monuments that talk of the past and modern shopping complexes that nod expectantly at the future. The town's achievement climaxed in being awarded the coveted Cultural Capital of Europe 2004. It all combines to make Lille an ideal short break destination.

Bon Voyage.

# Hopping Over

| FROM | TO | COMPANY | CROSSING TIME | FREQUENCY |
|---|---|---|---|---|
| **Folkestone** | **Calais Coquelles** | **Eurotunnel** Tel: 08705 353 535 No foot passengers Check in: 30 mins | 35 mins | Every 15 minutes |
| **Dover** | **Calais Port** | **Hoverspeed** Tel: 0870 5240 241 Check in: 30 mins | 60 mins | Hourly |
| | | **P&O Ferries** Tel: 08705 202 020 Check in: 30 mins | 75 mins | Every 45 mins at peak time |
| | | **SeaFrance** Tel: 08705 711 711 Check in: 45 mins | 90 mins | Every 90 mins at peak time |
| **Dover** | **Dunkirk** | **Norfolk Line** Tel: 0870 870 1020 Check in: 60  mins | 120 mins | Every 4 hours |
| **Waterloo London** | **Lille** | **Eurostar** **Most Direct route** Tel: 0870 1606600 Foot passengers only www.Eurostar.com Check in: 30 mins | 2 hours | Every 30-60 mins |

Directions:
From Calais take the A16/A26 motorway from Calais to Lille.

Driving time: 90 minutes

Further road travel information from:
Centre Régional d'Information Routière
Tel: 00 33 320 47 33 33

Directions: Take A25/A26 motorway from Dunkirk to Lille

Driving time: 90 mins

It's a 5 minute walk from the station to the old town.

# Hopping Over

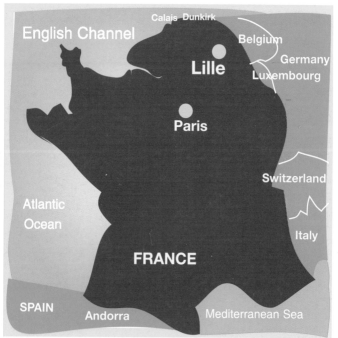

If you want to take your car, the fabulous motorways from Calais or Dunkirk direct to Lille means you can use any cross-Channel service and drive effortlessly to Lille in around an hour. Five motorway networks converge in Lille as follows: A1 to Paris, A27 to Brussels, A23 to Valenciennes, A22 to Amsterdam, A25 to Dunkirk changing to A26 to get to Calais. Go online for in-depth information www.info-route.com / www.autoroutes.fr

# Dover to Dunkerque

With up to 10 sailings a day Norfolkline is the smart way to cross the Channel.

Dunkerque is a favourite gateway into France that provides rapid access ...

...to Belgium, Holland and beyond.

SPECIAL OFFERS AVAILABLE THROUGHOUT THE YEAR

# Getting Around

*With its extensive public transport, getting around Lille is easy.*

Drivers will find the roads are well sign-posted making it reasonably easy to navigate the one-way systems. There is no free parking in Lille and anyway, onstreet parking is difficult. It is easier to use a car park. Otherwise, Lille has a very comprehensive network of transportation run by Transpole which can be picked up next to the Euralille complex. Here are the options:

## By Bus
The Transpole bus routes cover the whole metropolitan area. Catch one between the hours of 05.30 and 20.30.

## By Tram:
Two tramways head for Roubaix and Tourcoing giving acess to the designer shopping outlets of MacArthur Glen or L'Usine factory shops. Tram services run from 05.15 (06.10 weekends) to midnight.

## By VAL Métro
VAL métro is an extraordinary driverless train and the only one of its kind in the world. It is fully automated, and its routes are above and below the ground. The metro stations are graced with interesting works of art. There are 2 lines:

**Line 1** links Lille and Villeneuve d'Ascq

**Line 2** links Lomme to Roubaix and Tourcoing

## Travel at Night:
A network of night buses called the Clair de Lune operate in the Vieux Lille and heads out to other towns every half hour. Service starts at 21.30 and continues until 03.00. There are six routes in total, four leave the place des Buisses and two leave from place de la République.

Note: No public transport operates on May 1st.

# Getting Around

## Buying Tickets

There are ticket machines at every station and you can pay by credit card or with coins. A single ticket costs 1 euro and allows travel in one direction changing from métro to tram to bus as required. Carnets of 10 tickets are better value if you intend moving around and cost 10 euros. There are also one day tickets - Passe Journée - offering unlimited travel and cost around 3 euros.

A City Pass can be purchased which for 14 euros allows unlimited access to museums and attractions in Lille as well as unlimited travel. Information and help is avaiable at Lille-Flanders Station
Tel: 08 20 42 40 40.

## Taxi!

Taxis are found at the clearly marked taxi ranks and can be hailed in the street. There are two major ranks outside the two railway stations. To book Tel 03 20 06 06 / 03 20 06 64

## Sight Seeing Mini Bus

If you are short on time, take the sight seeing mini bus. The tour of Lille lasts around 1 hour and leave every hour from outside the tourist office on place Rihour. There is a really good multilingual audio-visual commentary to help you on the way. Tickets cost 7 euros and can be bought at the tourist office.

## Car Parking

There are ten pay-for large car parks in central Lille and some sought after pay-and-display parking zones. Free parking is avalable to shoppers at Carrefour hypermarket at the Eurolille shopping centre, but you do have to prove a certain spend.within Carrefour.

---

**TOURIST OFFICE**
**Office du**
**Tourisme**
**Palais Rihour**
**BP 205**
**59002 Lille Cedex**
**Tel: 00 33 (0) 320 21 94 21**
**Fax: 00 33( 0) 320 21 94 20**

Lille

RUE SOLFERINO

MASSENA

RUE DU MAL DE LATTRE DE TASSIGNY

BOUCHER DE PERTHIE

PLACE DE STRASBOURG

BOILEUX

RUE DE

RUE DE

AVENUE SQUARE FOCH

R D

RUE JEAN SANS PEUR

LELEU

RUE

ST ANDRE

RUE JACQUEMARS GIELEE

DE PUEBLA

BVD DE LA LIBERTE

RUE NATIONAL

P

RUE LEON GAMBETTA

RUE ALEX

RUE DU MAIRE

RUE

ST ETIENN

JEAN SANS PEUR

PERFECTURE

RUE JEAN SANS PEUR

RUE DE L'HOPITAL M

RUE PALAIS

RUE D'INKERMAN

RUE GOMBERT

RUE DE LA PICQUERIE

R P DUPONT

RUE DES F

PLACE DE LA REPUBLIQUE

RUE MAERTENS

RUE JGAUTHIER DE CHATILLON

P

PLACE RICHEBE

PLACE DE BETHUNE

RUE DE BETHUNE

R MOLF

PALAIS DES BEAUX ARTS

PLACE DU VIEUX MARCHE AUX CHEVAUX

R DU COURT DEBOUT

RUE DU BARBIER MAES

RUE J MAILLOTE

RUE DU PLAT

RUE DE MOLINEL

RUE D'AMIENS

BVD DE LA LIBERTE

RUE DE DELESTE

R OVIGNEUR

E LA VIGNETTE

AVE DU PRES J KENNEDY

RUE GUSTAVE DELORY

R LYDERIC

RUE MALPART

RUE DE PARIS

RUE DE PARIS

PORTE DE

*Lille, the capital of Flanders, has changed hands four times since 1066 and has been under siege on eleven different occasions!*

Once upon a time, the island of Insula was completely surrounded by marshland; and every year the marshes would be covered in an abundance of lilies.

By 300AD the sea had risen too much and certain drastic measures had to be taken to reclaim the land. With the help of the monks and in due course the Counts of Flanders, they built dykes to control the waters and then built powerful windmills to shoo the waters back into the sea.

Sufficiently tamed, the waters became manageable; canals were developed and cargo was easily transported. Through sheer blood, sweat and tears, the barren land became extremely fertile.

Though the marshland disappeared, the lily flower that thrived so well on the marshes, was adopted as a symbol of the people. It was named 'Fleur de Lille' and was awarded a special place on the coat of arms of the City. In 1066 the island became known as L'isle,

### Turbulent Times

The first reference to Lille appeared in 1066 in a charter donated by Baudoin V, the Count of Flanders, to the collegiate church. He referred to it as L'isle - the island. In fact the count's castle was built on an island in the Deûle River and for two centuries, while trade with England and Northern Europe was prospering, the town and port developed around it. The site of the port is now **avenue du Peuple-Belge**.

During this time of prosperity the King of France took a great interest in the city. In 1214, during the Battle of

Bouvines, King Phillippe Auguste defeated the Count of Flanders. He in turn abandoned his thrown, leaving it to his wife the Countess Jeanne.

Since then, Lille has had a turbulent history, during which it has undergone a change of nationality four times, faced eleven sieges and has been destroyed several times.

In 1369 Philip the Bold made Flanders part of the duchy of Burgundy after his dynastic marriage to Marguerite of Flanders.

Just over a hundred years later the last Duke of Burgundy, Charles the Bold died and his heiress Marie of Burgundy married Maximillian of Austria, thereby giving control of the duchy of Burgundy, which included Lille, to the Hapsburgs.

As the years spilled into the next century, the duchy became Spanish when Charles V of Spain became emperor thereby incorporating Lille into the the Spanish Netherlands.

Through yet another marriage, Lille's status changed again when it became French catalytically through the marriage of Maria-Theresa of Spain and Louis XIV. In 1667, believing his marriage gave him rights to Lille, Louis XIV besieged Lille relentlessly for nine days emerging victorious. He soon made Lille the capital of the Northern provinces. Shortly afterwards he enlarged the town, and took measures to protect his winnings.

He commissioned Vauban to build a star-shaped **citadel** dubbed 'the Queen of Citadels'. He then laid down some laws to regulate the height and style of the houses.

Over a century later, in 1792, Lille was under siege again, this time by the Austrians. An epic David and Goliath style battle was fought - the Austrians were fortified with some 35,000 troops and Lille was defended by just one small garrison. Cannon-balls were used by the Austrians in an effort of earnest destruction. Some cannon-balls achieved their goal of destruction, others lodged themselves in the brickwork of the buildings. These can still be seen today on the buildings at **Rang Beauregards**. They are regarded as historical monuments and are owned by the City and not the owners of the buildings. They serve as a constant reminder of how the valiant inhabitants of Lille held on until the Austrians raised the siege.

In 1914 Lille was taken over by Bavarians who in just three fiercely bloody days of resistance destroyed 900 buildings.

On receiving the surrender, prince Ruprecht of Bavaria refused the sword of Captain de Pardieu "in recognition of the heroism of the French troops".

The French had to capitulate yet again on 1st of June 1940, during the Second World War, to the Germans. Again the French held on for three days of bloody resistance but Rommel's tanks and seven German divisions proved too much for them.

Today, the only invasion Lille sustains is a healthy flow of tourists.

*The Star Shaped Citadel is not just a fortification
- it is a self-contained town*

Louis XIV, the Sun King, having just conquered the town of Lille, wished to fortify it with a Citadelle. He commissioned Sébastien Leprestre, Marquis of Vauban to build it just outside Vieux Lille. It was constructed with an impressive speed in just three years between 1667 and 1670 and remains the largest and the best preserved citadel in France. Construction of this amazing fortification proved to be quite a feat involving 60 million newly baked bricks and the efforts of 2000 men.

The outer moats were used as execution sites during World War I and II and many French patriots were shot.

It is in fact a small self-contained town surrounded by five bastions, and five demi-lune (half moon) fortifications in a star formation - a design

## CITADELLE

ADDRESS:
avenue du 42ème Régiment
d'Infantrie.
59000
TELEPHONE:
Tourist office 03 20 2194 21

OPEN HOURS
Visitors can take a guided tour of the citadelle on Sundays from 15.00 to 17.00  between May-August and on selected dates outside this period.
You must book in advance and no impromptu visits are allowed. Contact the tourist office to arrange a visit.

There is ample space for wheelchairs but the streets are cobbled and may prove a little bumpy.

COST: 7 euros.

GETTING THERE:
**Métro** to Gare Lille Flandres, then line 1 to République.
**Bus** 14 to Jardin Vauban

which later inspired the US Pentagon. It can house up to 1,200 soldiers and there are usually around 1000 soldiers and foreign legionnaires at any one time. Historically, uniforms include the naval badges since the first regiment stationed here were marines.

The main entrance is at the gabled Porte Royale. The gate acts as a potent symbol of the monarchy and indeed of France. The façade is inscribed with Latin and the drawbridge is angled from the 4m-thick walls in order to evade enemy fire.

Every year in April, 14 of the 28 northern fortresses hold an open day, but usually the public are only permitted to visit this working garrison an official guided tour.

Vauban's original models of the citadel are displayed at the Palais des Beaux Arts.

Citadelle & Bois de Boulogne

### *An amazing park, surrounded by the water of the Deûle river and still within the city limits*

Town and country exist in tandem within Lille's city limits. One hundred and twenty five hectares of the Bois de Boulogne contain a mix of wild and not so wild life including prowling panthers, monkeys, soldiers,a variety of keep fit fanatics and picnickers.

The park entirely wraps itself around the **citadelle** and is in turn contained within a loop of the river **Deûle** offering pretty lock gates of the **Ecluse de la Barre**. Within the expanse of lovely greenery are picturesque towpaths and a free-to-enter zoo complete with an Isle de Singes - an island filled with monkeys - rhinos, panthers and zebras.

A nearby playground with dodgems, side-shows and candy floss stands keeps the children amused.

Just outside the zoo is a cobbled pathway which forms part of the notoriously difficult annual (every April) Paris to Roubaix cycle race. Locals refer to this stretch as 'the Hell of the North'.

At the entrance of the park is a tree-line Esplanade, land-scaped by Vauban himself in 1675. Sunday mornings sees a myriad of joggers; some follow the signposted exercise circuit around the fortifications through the ramparts and willow trees. They are joined by Foreign Legionnaire who are distinguishable by their blue track suits. The Esplanade continues across the canal at the **Pont de Ramponneau** heading to the **Champs de Mars** where the festive funfairs pitch their attractions at each of the

### BOIS DE BOULOGNE

ADDRESS:
Surrounds the Citadelle
TELEPHONE:
Tourist office 03 20 2194 21

OPEN HOURS
Anyone can visit daily. On
Sunday mornings there tends to
be a joggers rushhour.
During the French school
holidays there are funfairs too.

ZOO
Avenue Mathias Delobel
59000
TELEPHONE:
03 28 52 07 00

ZOO OPEN HOURS
Mon-Fri 09.00-17.00 (Apr-Oct)
10-00-16.30 (Nov-Mar)
Sat-Sun and public holidays
09.00-18.30 (Apr-Oct)
09.00-16.30 (Nov-Mar)
Closed 2nd Sunday in Dec to
2nd Sunday in Feb.

Entry is free

GETTING THERE:
**Bus** 14 to Jardin Vauban

French school holidays.
On a sober note, visitors might
take a moment to visit the
Félix Desruelle's Monument
aux Fusillées located at the
edge of the Bois at the Square
Daubenton. It commemorates
the untimely deaths of the
Lillois members of the French
Resistance victims shot by the
Nazis against the walls of the
Citadelle. The area
was formerly moat house, but
now is home to a grass lawn.

### LA PORTE DE ROUBAIX
### Rue de Roubaix

It was at the now run-down Porte de Roubaix in 1972 when an Austrian major armed with just an ultimatum of the Duke of Saxe-Eschen, vainly demanding the city's surrender. To the left of the gate is a 17th century house - 'House of Old Men". Today its location near the Lille Europe train station marks the end of the old town and the beginning of Euralille.

### LA PORTE DE GAND
### Rue de Gand

This, the last fortified gate to Lille, stands next to rue de Gand overseeing the cobbled streets and restaurants at the fashionable end of the city. Its archway and coloured brick are appealing and the windows at the top look into a restarant and look over the gate's gardens.

Both the gates of Roubaix and Gand were built during Spanish Occupation of the city. When trams made their debut in Lille in 1875, both gates were opened to allow access for them. Since then their moats have been turned into gardens.

### LA PORTE DE PARIS
### place Simon Vollant

The gate which served as an 'Arc de Triomphe', (though much smaller), was constructed between 1685 and1692 in honour of the capture of Lille by Louis XIV.

The arch is decorated with the Coat of Arms of Lille (bearing one lily) and the Coat of Arms of France (bearing 3 lilies). The top of the arch is crowned with two angels whose role is to tell the world about the Sun King's conquest. The portal has a statue of Hercules - symbol of strength - on the right, and Mars, the god of war, on the left  Place Simon Vollant was named after the architect of the Porte de Paris.

## *In the heart of Lille the 'Grand Place' has always been a grand place*

Probably the busiest area in Lille, is the **Grand' Place** in the heart of Central Lille. The official name for the square is **Place du Général de Gaulle**, for it was here in 1890 that Général de Gaulle, a former French president, was born.

Lille's Coat of Arms over the Grand Place entrance of the Bourse

Originally, the square was used as a bustling wheat market place back in the 11th century. These days, the beautifully preserved historic buildings surrounding the square, together with its myriad of cafés and terraces, still makes an obvious place to rendez-vous and a good place to commence any sight-seeing tour. Around the square there are a number of very impressive buildings.

---

**HOW TO GET FROM THE LILLE-EUROPE TRAN STATION TO THE GRANDE PLACE ON FOOT**

Exit the trains station and turn left, past Euralille shopping centre. Continue past the Lille-Flanders station. Cross the road at traffic lights before the fountains (opposite the Napoleon restaurant). Turn right into rue Faidherbe. Continue past the Opera House and cut through the Bourse - the old stock exchange. Come out at the other end of the courtyard to **Grande Place- Place du General de Gaulle**.

The most beautiful is the **Vieille Bourse**, the old stock exchange. It was built by Julien Destrée in 1653 whose commission was to build an exchange to rival that of any great city. It was also a commission motivated greatly by the persistent ill-health of the Lillois bankers and merchants. Trading had always taken place in the unprotected open air at the **Fontaine-au-Change** on the **Place du Vieux-Marché** in all types of weather. As a result the bankers endured regular bouts of flu and colds. By 1651 they had had enough and took their wheezy deputation to the Magistrate. The magistrate in sympathy with their cause put in an application to Philip IV, King of Spain and Count of Flanders for a more suitable stock exchange. The result is a quadrangle of 24 - privately purchased-ornately decorated yet identical houses

surrounding an interior rectangular courtyard where trading could take place. Access is through any one of the four arches located at each of the four sides.

There are three levels to the houses. The ground floor was reserved for and tenanted by stylish shops chosen for their ability to complement the overall beauty of the decor rather than utility. The wealth of Flemish Renaissance style

decoration includes cute chubby cherubs, garlands and masks around the windows. The four entrances are marked with cornucopias, symbolic of wealth and happiness; Turkish turbanned heads tell of their Eastern markets and the Lions of Flanders signify that Lille once belonged to the Netherlands. Under the arcades there are medallions and tablets in honour of great men of science.

Unfortunately with the passage of time, the Bourse became dilapidated and had to undergo serious restoration. The task was undertaken by two dozen big Northern enterprises such as Auchan, La Redoute and Le Crédit du Nord - the biggest restoration project of private sponsorship ever known in France. Below the windows on the second floor are the colourful emblems of these sponsors.

No longer used as the stock exchange, these days the courtyard houses second-hand booksellers' stalls and florists and a band of chess players. The current champion, François,a bookseller, says that any passer-by or tourist is welcome to participate. Opposite the Vielle Bourse is **Le Furet du Nord,** Europe's biggest book shop. The building in which it is located is a copy of a 17th century house.

**LILLE AT NIGHT**
Every Wednesday during July and August, meet at the foot of the Déese fountain at 9pm for a walking tour of Vieux Lille after dark. The tour ends with a beer tasting.

**The Goddess** statue stands tall on her column, **La Colonne de la Déesse**, rising up in the middle of the **Grand Place** (Place du Général de Gaulle) from the midst of a fountain.

She stands in memory of the Austrian canon ball siege that took place in 1792. Despite the onslaught of 35,000 Austrian soldiers the townsfolk bravely stood their ground and were victorious. Initially she was to be placed on top of Arc de Triomphe in Paris but she returned to Lille, standing in place Rihour for three years before being moved in 1845 to stand atop Charles Benvignat's column on the Grand'Place.

Her crown represents Lille's ramparts amd in her right hand she holds the fuse which fired the old canons and her left hand points to the inscription on the pedestal:

*'the courageous refusal of Mayor André of Lille to surrender the town'*.

The column, which was erected in 1845, was designed by the architect Charles Benvignat and the sculpture of the goddess was the work of Theodore Bra of Douai.

Throughout the year she will witness a variety of activities taking place below her such as student protests, bands playing in the Gay Pride Days, parading giants during the Fêtes de Lille and at Christmas a grotto is created and stays throughout December and January. A huge ferris wheel accompanies Christmas and turns continuously from early morning and well into the small hours. Otherwise, a quiet day would see countless people just milling around using her as a landmark.

There are three more female statues around the square. They can be seen crowning the top of the **Voix du Nord** (the voice of the North) newspaper building. These

golden statues were placed on the 1932 headquarters by architect Victor Laprade to defy the wind and weather. Each of the three graces represents the region's Northern provinces of Artois, Flanders and Hainault. The building is further steeped in symbolism, perhaps of a boastful type.

The frontage has 28 windows which are a very visual representation of the 28 issues of the newspaper that are printed. Next to La Voix du Nord is the 16th century **Grand'Garde**. This was originally built to house the king's guards, but now it is used as a theatre called **La Métaphore**.

Take a look at the buildings behind the Vielle Bourse by turning into **Rue des Manneliers** (the basket makers road) or **Rue des Sept Agaches** (road of 7 magpies) on either side of the Vieille Bourse. Both these roads lead to **Place du Théâtre** situated at the start of **Boulevard Carnot.**

**The Place du Théâtre** became the venue of the new chamber of commerce, **Nouvelle Bourse**, in 1903. It was built by Louis Cordonnier in the new-Flemish style architecture. The Bourse comes complete with its own bell tower looming over the building and in fact over the city. The 100 metres high bellfry symbolises the power of industrial cities.

The neighbouring building is the **Opera**, originally built in 1785, but accidentally burnt down in 1903. The sumptuously decorated replacement was built by Louis Cordonnier in the Louis XVI style. Its inauguration took place 1923 during which Lalo, Bizet and Massenet had top billing. On the pediment there are figures of Apollo and muses To the left is an allegorical music band representing music, and to the right is a tragedy sculpted by Lemaire.

Facing the chamber of commerce is the **Rang de Beauregard**, a uniform row of elegant terraced houses. These were built in 1687 by order of the Magistrate of Lille, to complement the architectural style of the Chamber of Commerce building.

The three-storey houses built only in brick and stone are decorated with pilasters and cartouches and are the most characteristic examples of 17th century architecture in the area. In similar fashion to the Vieille Bourse, the ground floor is home to very elegant shops.

Take a moment to scrutinise the walls and search out small cannon balls lodged in the brickwork. These are in fact the canon balls left by the Austrians during their siege some 200 years earlier.

Though the buildings may be privately owned, the balls are deemed historical monuments and belong to the city.

*Fifty metres beyond the Heart of Lille
lies a new urban district designed
to be at the forefront of
technological chic*

If your vision of the future or even modern life includes glass dominated structures, spacious walk-ways, and high rise tower blocks, then Euralille may meet with with your idea of technological chic.

It certainly met with Mr Mauroy's vision, the chairman of the urban development. He has been quoted as saying *'Trains go everywhere and cows look at them. They do nothing for the economic development. Euralille will.'*

At Place de l'Europe, looking to your left from Le Corbusier Viaduct, is the **Lille-Europe train station**. Its function is to service travellers between Paris and London using the Channel Tunnel for high-speed train services to other French destinations - such as Lille.

The structure has been described by its architect J.M. Duthilleul as *'a new model of the station which reconciles the train and the citizen'.*

Certainly the 400 metre long window facade of the station allows train spotters to delight in the view of the high speed TGV trains. Another 15 metre high facade leads the way into the centre of town.

The station is linked to **Lille-Flandres train station** by a viaduct with four arches and the area acts as a central point for all transport facilities such as the VAL metro and the main roads.

EUROLILLE
ADDRESS: Avenue le Courbusier
TELEPHONE: 03 20 14 52
All buses and trams can be caught from here.
It is located between the two train stations

There are two emerging glass structured towers. The smaller of the two is the Tour de Crédit Lyonnais, designed by Christian de Portzampac to symbolise renewal. It has been affectionately nicknamed 'the pinball machine'. The second, spanning 25 floors is called Tour Lilleurope'.

The exterior of the huge Centre Euralille shopping centre is entirely made from glass, topped with a wedge shaped flat roof described by its architect as *'a sort of metallic puff pastry'*. Though very modern, there is a look of severity about it.To the south, hidden behind the tower is the oval shaped Lille Grand-Palais, which is used as the town's exhibition hall and conference centre and can seat 5,000 people.

Within the futuristic landscape, a new park has been conceived. Park Henri-Matisse has been designed over twenty acres and stretches almost as far as the ancient Port de Roubaix: the gateway where old Lille meets the new. The plants and foliage are still in their infancy, but the park is still a fine place to take a stroll.

*The elegant fine arts museum was opened in 1997 by President Chirac after seven years of restoration.*

Lille's Fine Arts museum is regarded highly in France as second only to the Louvre in Paris. The building itself is a fine 19th century example and houses a prestigious collection of European paintings. A superb staircase leads you to masterpieces by Rubens, van Dyck, Goya (in particular **Youth and Age**), the Medea of Delacroix , Courbet's **Après Diner à Omans** and forty drawings by Raphaêl. 17th and 18th century ceramics and cabinets can be seen as well as totally restored works from the Middle Ages and the Renaissance. Rich red walls and floppy chairs conspire to keep you there and there is a lot to see so allow about two hours.

PALAIS DES BEAUX-ARTS
ADDRESS:
place de la République 59000
TELEPHONE: 03 20 06 78 00
Guided tours: 03 20 06 78 17

OPEN HOURS: Mon 14.00-18.00
Wed to Thurs Fri 10.00 to 19.00
Closed public holidays.

MÉTRO: République

*This 13th century hospital is now a museum,
faithfully protraying life in Lille during
15th-17th centuries*

You have to look behind the old shopfronts of of the oldest street in the city - rue de la Monnaie -  to find the discretely located Musée de 'LHospice Comtesse.

It was founded in 1237, as a hospital and hospice for the needy by Jeanne of Constantinople, Countess of Flanders as a charitable gesture.

Now a museum, it depicts  the development  of builder's art from 15th to 17th century. You can visit the sick bay, the kitchen where there are hundreds of Lille tiles, the chapel and the former nuns' dormitory to view the Dutch and Flemish paintings.  Also on show are wood carvings and tapestries by Guillaume Werniers, the famous Lille weaver.There is  an ancient and very rare collection of musical instruments and popular music, called the Hel collection.

The museum gives off an agreeable air of spirituality and peace.

---

MUSÉE DE L'HOSPICE
COMTESSE
ADDRESS:
32 rue de la Monnaie 59000
TELEPHONE: 03 28 36 84 00

OPEN HOURS: Mon 14.00-18.00
Wed to Thurs Fri 10.00 to 12.30
Closed Tues & public
holidays.and Braderie weekend

MÉTRO: Lion D'or or Gare
Flanders
BUSES 3,6,9

ENTRY: 2 euros
Free for children under 12.
Free entry 1st Sun of every
month
Free guided tour4s are available

*The works of the greatest artists of the last 150 years can be viewed in the galleries and the gardens of this cultural park at Villneuve d'Asq*

Lille's University campus suburb at Villeneuve d'Asq has an surprising cultural attraction - the Musée d'Art Moderne. The building is pretty humble but consists of the works of the most influential painters of each of the major art movements all in their own galleries. Included are six works by Picasso including **Musical Instruments** and **Death Head;**. Bracque's **Maison et Arbres**, Rouault, Miro and Masson and a canvass by Modigliani **Assis à la Chemise**. The Fauvist and Cubist rooms tend to be the most popular.

Works by contemporary artists are also on display. Among them are Eduardo Arroyo, Richard Deacon, François Dufrène and Dennis Oppenheim.

Outside large sculptures are found here and there and include Picasso's Femme aux Bras Ecartés. Through the huge glass windows which gives over to the display, you can see strollers and cyclists casually making their way through the art.

MUSÉE D'ART MODERNE
ADDRESS:
1 allée du Musée 59650 Villeneuve D'Asq
TELEPHONE: 03 20 19 68 68
OPEN HOURS: Wed-Mon 10.00-18.00.Closed 1 Jan, 1 May, 25 Dec

MÉTRO: 2 to gare Lille Flandres, then line 1 to Pont de Bois, then bus 41 to Parc urbain-Musée and follow the footpatch to the park.

ENTRY: Fee applies
Free entry 1st Sun of each month.

## MUSÉE DES CANNONIERS

ADDRESS: 44 rue des Cannoniers, 59000
TEL: 03 20 55 58 90
OPEN HOURS: Wed,Thurs,Sat,Sun 14.00-17.00. closed holidays, first 3 weeks Aug, 15 Dec-15 Feb.
ENTRY: 4.50 euros
From Gare Lille Flanders walk through the Parc Matisse through the Porte de Roubaix to rue de Roubaix. Turn right into rue des Cannoniers, second right into rue des Urbanistes.

## MUSÉE D'HISTOIRE NATURELLE ET MUSÉE GÉOLOGY

ADDRESS: 19 rue de Bruxelles
TEL: 03 28 55 30 80
OPEN HOURS: Wed-Fri 9.00-12.00, 14.00-17.00, Sun 10.00-17.00 Closed Tue, Sat.
ENTRY: Free midweek 2.4 euros Sun.
METRO: République
BUS: 13 from Gare Flandres to Jeanne Arc

## MAISON NATALE ET MUSÉE GÉNÉRALE DE GAULLE

ADDRESS: 9 rue Princess, 59000
TEL: 03 28 38 12 05
OPEN HOURS: Wed-Sun 10.00-12.00 and 14.00-17.00
BUS: 3 or 6 from Gare Flandres to Magazin. Take rue St-André to rue Princesse.

## MUSÉE DES CANNONIERS SÉDENTAIRES DE LILLE

Lille is a garrison town, so it is right that it should have a military museum.

This museum, a former Urbanistes convent is full of artillery with more than 3000 weapons, documents and maps from 1777 to 1945 and more than 100 canons. Canon enthusiasts will be able to enthuse over the impressive 1765 Gribeauval canon presented by the First Consul who later became the Emperor Napoléon.

## MUSÉE D'HISTOIRE NATURELLE ET MUSÉE GÉOLOGY

The Natural History Museum has an abundance of mammals, whale skeletons hanging from the ceiling stuffed birds, reptiles and insects together with rocks and fossils.

## MAISON NATALE ET MUSÉE GÉNÉRAL DE GAULLE

Charles de Gaulle was born here, in his grandmother's house opposite Eglise St-

André on November 22 1890. The house is now a museum dedicated to him and contains childhood souvenirs including his Christening robe and tracks his career as a soldier, Free French army leader and President of France.Also documented is de Gaulle's refusal to accept Marshall Pétain's 1940 truce with Nazi Germany and his historic speech in the same year, broadcast from London to rally the French army.
A Citroen DS car complete with bullet holes is on display - this is the car he was travelling in outside Paris when a failed assasination attempt was made on his life.

### NOTRE DAME DE LA TREILLE

This amazing church had its foundations laid in 1854, the edifice completed towards the end of the 19th century but in 1947 work came to a complete halt as funds had run out. Until 1999 the front entrance was boarded up but new funding was found and the magnificent entrance was finally finished. It all looks very new age but the fantastic window by Kijno produces fabulous lighting effects inside.

NOTRE DAMME DE LA TREILLE
ADDRESS: place Gilleson
OPEN HOURS: Hours vary.

BUS 3,6 or 9 from Gare Flanders to Lion d'Or.Take rue de la Monnaie then first left to pl Gilleson

*Within walking distance, there is
the biggest bookshop in Europe,
the most beautiful fish shop in France
and the oldest sweet shop in Lille.*

*What's more, there's Folklore galore !*

### THE P'TIT QUINQUIN STATUE

At the entrance of Square Foch stands a statue in memory of Alexandre Desrousseaux, author of the famous lullaby **P'tit Quinquin**. It was composed in 1853 yet, most people in Lille will know at least a few words of this very tragic song. It is a story about a poor lacemaker who has resigned herself to a hopeless life and trying to lull her baby to sleep. To the left of the statue are the woman's tools of her trade and to the right is her crying child.

The tune was played at the poet's funeral. The tune that now heralds the TGV train announcements and the chime of the Nouvelle Bourse are made up of the first five notes of the lullaby. The sculpture of this fine statue is the work of Eugene Deplechin.

### VOLTAIRE WAS HERE!
#### Rue de la Vieille Comédie

The 'road of the old comedy' - is so called because this is the very site that Voltaire premiered his production of 'Mahomet' in 1741.

### INTERIORS

A good indication of how young the Lillois population is, has to be the abundance of interior decor shops most with the words 'Wedding List' emblazoned on the front doors.

Incidentally..

The Lillois have been nicknamed **'Ch'ti'** by their counterparts elsewhere in France because their accent is phonetically similar to the sound 'ch'ti'

### THE BIGGEST BOOK SHOP IN EUROPE

Le Furet du Nord at 15 place du Général du Gaulle is allegedly the largest book shop in Europe. It covers 8000 square metres over eight floors, housing over 500,000 titles as well as a vast range of music and games.

Of course if you speak French, you have a fabulous choice of reading and listening material to choose. If not, the shop is worth visiting just to see the clever tangle of the aerial footbridges and staircases.

### RYSSELS

Ryssel is a Flemish word which means Lille. It also signifies a little bit of chocoholic luxury: These pralines are covered in milk chocolate - you crunch them first and then let them melt in the mouth. You can buy them at a confisserie. Try Conifserie Yanka, 10 rue de la Monnaie.

### L'HUÎTRIÈRE rue des Chat Bossus

Is this the most beautiful poissonnerie (fish monger) in France?

Unchanged since 1928, its mosaic decor in vibrant colours - the work of Mathurin Meheut - the maritime motifs in blue and gold and its columns decorated with porcelain are all inspired by the Art Déco style. They have been widely admired for a century. The glass stained windows and mosaic panels continue the maritime theme.

The attached restaurant is considered the best in Lille but it does have prices to match.

## The Insights

### MEERT PATISSERIE

This beautiful outlet on **27 rue Esquermoise** is the oldest sweet shop in France. The description 'sweet shop' is a little unfair, as it does not portray the quality of the confectionery, saying nothing about its copper mouldings, cast-iron lace balconies and gallery in gilded filigree. Dating from 1760 it was favoured by Charles de Gaulle who regularly ordered Gauffres (waffles biscuits) and enjoyed them 'with great pleasure'. In 1849 the Belgian royal family awarded their Royal Warrant to Monsieur Meert.The quaint tea room at the rear of the shop offers over a hundred teas and a fine selection of pastries and savoury snacks. A pot of tea and cake costs around 6 euros.

### LA GARE LILLE-FLANDERS TRAIN STATION

This train station, Lille's oldest, was originally built in Paris in 1846 and known as the **Gare du Nord.** When the inauguration train arrived in Lille from Paris carrying government ministers and two royal princes, it was greeted by the Mayor, blessed by the Bishop and composer Hector Berlioz wrote a song for it called 'Song of the Iron Roads' which premiered that day.

Amazingly, twenty years later the Gare du Nord was dismantled stone by stone and rebuilt in Lille. Another floor was added to accommodate the clock. Rue Faidherbe links the station to the town centre.

---

### TIME OUT BY THE RIVER

In 1066, Baudoin V, the Count of Flanders, lived in the castrum encircled by the waters of the Deûle. The castle is long gone but the calm waters of the river Deûle offer apleasant 680km tour of the Flemish countryside. Departure is from Lille on a canoe or a barge. Ask at the tourist office
Tel: Tourisme Fluviale on 03 20 14 57 57

**THE LEGEND OF THE GIANTS**

Flanders is renowned for its traditional, colourful giants which are brought out and paraded in the streets during holidays. Its a skilled tradition, as the giants have to be sturdy enough to cope with being exhibited and danced with, and light enough to be portable.

At the last count there were around 200 giants, all based on fabulous heroes or animals of legendary repute.

Lille itself has its own indigenous giants, who having been created in 1999, are newcomers. Their names are Phinaert and Lydéric.

According to legend, Phinaert was a highwayman living in AD 600 who lived in a château upon which site Lille now stands. One night he attacked the Prince of Dijon and his pregnant wife on their way to England.

Phinaert killed the prince but the prince's wife escaped and managed to give birth to her son before being caught again by the highwayman.

The baby was brought up by a hermit who baptised him Lydéric. When he had reached adulthood Lydéric sought to avenge the death of his parents and challenged Phinaert to a duel and promptly slew him.

He went on to marry the daughter of King Dagobert and the Flemish forest which had once belonged to Phinaert fell under his jurisdiction.

*Imagine spending an entire weekend walking the streets, buying second hand items and eating mussels and fries.*
*Thousands of people shop this way every year.*

Commercial acumen is rife in Lille. From the humble honey roasted peanut vendor who appears at sunset to imbue the evening air with sweet aromas to the classy high fashion shops with fabulously decorated windows. But no shopping experience can offer the excitement and fun of the annually held braderies.

### THE BRADERIE:
**WWW.BRADERIE-LILLE.COM**
In the middle ages, servants won the right to sell their masters' old and unwanted clothes and jumble on the streets of Lille. The sale lasted from sunset to sunrise and proved so popular that eventually the masters joined in. The event soon established itself as an annual event. The tradition still lives on in the form of the modern day '**braderie**', - a word which

lamely translates as '**jumble sale**'. On the first weekend of September, Lille becomes a giant flea market. Over 200 km of sidewalks and doorways are

overrun by stalls, trestles and pitches.. For thirty-three hours non-stop cars are banned and the streets become pedestrianised areas packed with local people and visitors buying and selling their second-hand goods. Vendors vary from professional boot-sale traders, antique dealers to ordinary people selling unwanted items. Even the metro runs throughout the night ensuring everyone can come and get home and you can be sure that every hotel room is booked during this period.

Anything and everything goes and people come from all over Europe to join the giant non-stop shopping party.

Traditionally, hundreds of tons of mussels, fries and merguezes (thin sausages) are consumed. Throughout the event, the empty mussel shells create ever enlarging mountains. Though this creates an ever increasing whiff of the sea, there is an element of pride for the stall or restaurant which has managed to gather the biggest mound of shells.

### GENERAL MARKETS

Lille has a very good array of general and antique markets and they are the best places to buy the freshest local produce including, vegetables, cheese direct from the dairy, andouillettes, - sausages - chicory and endives.

Regional products are brought in from the all over Nord-Pas-de-Calais.

WAZEMMES FLEA MARKET
The biggest of the markets is the **Wazemmes flea market** located in a central working class residential area at **Quartier de Wazemmes: Place Nouvelle Aventure** - New Adventures square. You meet it head on as you emerge from Gambetta métro station.

This huge market takes an otherwise ordinary district and transforms it into a very busy, atmospheric and vibrant hive

WAZEMMES FLEA MARKET
ADDRESS: place de la Nouvelle Aventure, 59000
OPEN HOURS: Sun, Tues, Thurs mornings

MÉTRO République. Metro 2 to Gare Lille Flandres then line 1 to Gambetta

of lively activity every Sunday, Tuesday and Thursday mornings.

The Eglise St Pierre-St-Paul, is conveniently located in the

hub of all the activities where, no doubt, locals can receive a good dose of spiritual sustenance, before venturing into the marketplace for their physical sustenance. But they will have to pass the antique dealers who congregate just in front of the church. They then have to pass the florists in front of the covered market enjoying a burst of colour and sweet aromas thrown out by the flowers from the Flemish , Belgian and Dutch countryside. At last they get to the covered market where lunch and dinner is waiting for them: vegetables, meat and seafood are on offer.

Elsewhere in the market the flea element flourishes as second hand clothes, books and various items of junk are disposed of.

Though most shops in Lille are closed on Sundays, the shops located in the area around **rue Leon Gambetta**, remain open taking advantage of the extra trade brought to them by the Wazemmes market.

### OTHER MARKETS

**Marché du Concert place du Concert**
This general food market is open Wednesdays, Fridays and Sundays.

**Marché Sébastopol Place Sébastopol**
Another general market open on Wednesdays and Saturdays.

**Vieille Bourse place de Général de Gaulle**
Every day flowers and books are on sale alongside each other within the sanctuary of the courtyard of the magnificent Vieille Bourse - the old stock exchange.

**Petit Marché de L'Art rue Leon Trulin**
A twice-monthly Saturday morning art market which takes place alongside the opera house. Local artis display the fruits f their labour on the 1st and 3rd Saturday of the month.

*The best shopping in Lille is all within a defined walkable area from the Grand'Place. With so much to choose from, the question remains:*

### Is Lille the ultimate in Retail Therapy?

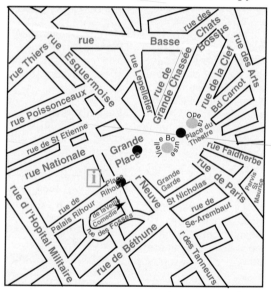

Everywhere you look there is somewhere inviting to go shopping in Lille. It seems every designer retailer has an outlet in the heart of Lille.

Major names such as the hypermarket Auchan and La Redoute mail order company have their origins here. Cartier, Louis Vuitton, Yves St Laurent amongst others, grace the roads with their stylish presence, especially in **rue Esquermoise**.

Throughout the city there are specialist shops selling art, interior decorative ornaments, ethnic memorabilia, pens, out-there jewellery, fragrant soaps and anything else you care to think of. It is a pleasure to get lost in a city where shopping is an adventure.

In fact there are so many places to shop within one definable walking area in Lille, it is hard to know where to flash your credit card first.

The **Grand' Place** (otherwise known as **place du Général du Gaulle**) is probably a good place to start then turning into rue **Grande Chausée** leading off from the square where stylish shops are prolific. Our overview starts at Grande'Place also known as Place du Général de Gaulle:

### PLACE DU GÉNÉRAL DU GAULLE

### Le Furet du Nord
**15 place du Général du Gaulle**
**Tel: 03 20 78 43 43**
This is the most famous book store in France, reputedly Europe's biggest. Thousands of books, magazines and cds are available.

### Esprit
**17 place du Général du Gaulle**
**Tel: 03 20 31 88 19**
A spacious clothes boutique for women. The modern and sportswear garments are Esprit's own label.

From the **Grand' Place** make your way to **rue de la Grande Chaussée**.

### RUE DE LA GRANDE CHAUSSÉE

### Dormeuil
**6 rue de la Grande Chaussée**
**Tel: 03 20 55 88 83**
One hundred and fifty years of trading have made this outlet a

bit of an institution. Although fashioned of old it is not old fashioned. The men's wear is inspired by Italian fashion and rather trendy.

### Hermès
**8 rue de la Grande Chaussée**
**Tel: 03 20 51 44 51**
Oh those famous scarves! Hermes has won the accolade of having the highest turnover in France after the Parisien branch. In recognition of its success it has been granted an opulent leather staircase.

### Caroline Biss
**13-15 rue de la Grande Chaussée**
**Tel: 03 20 21 09 19**
Women will fall in love with the elegant, quality clothes and accessories. Serious shoppers can sip coffee as they empty their purse.

### El Caballo
**20 rue de la Grande Chaussée**
**Tel: 03 28 04 57 74**
You know you have entered

Spanish territory simply by the background music playing. The sombreros and Flamencos are a give-away too. There is also a range of leather goods, hunting and fishing gear and day wear imported from Spain

### Faconnable
**21 rue de la Grande Chaussée**
**Tel: 03 20 06 28 00**
This unisex clothes shop sells 'prêt a porter' suits for men and a range of day wear for women.

### La Botte Chantilly
**22/24 rue de la Grande Chaussée**
**Tel: 03 20 55 46 41**
This shoe shop has been owned by the Roos family since 1992 and is known locally for its quality branded shoes. The range here includes children's shoes from Start-rite and Clarkes amid others such as Timberland. There is added value at this outlet as not only can you buy

shoes here but you can also discover a little history at the same time.

Behind the shop is the house in which the famous Musketeer D'Artagnan lived when he was the Governor of Lille in 1672. Just look through the rear glass walls and you will be able to see it. Its location being one layer away from the main road is significant as only important people could afford to live in locations set back from the noisy roads.

### Laura Ashley
**25 rue de la Grande Chaussée**
On sale are pretty wall papers, paints and decorative items on the first floor. The ground floor has clothes and hats in the distinctive Laura Ashley style.

### Pavillon Christofle
**48 rue de la Grande Chaussée**
**Tel: 03 28 51 46 20**
Christofle are famous for the luxurious dining adornments.

Crystal offerings, cutlery, table linen and crockery. It's all here.

### Louis Vuitton
**29 rue de la Grande Chaussée**
Specialise in their branded leather bags but where £100 may buy you a purse.with the famous LV insignia.

### Kenzo
**52 rue de la Grande Chaussée**
**Tel: 03 20 51 78 79**
This huge, trendy outlet offers music and a relaxed shopping atmosphere. Clothes are hip or sporty.

At the end of turn right into **rue des Chats Bossus -** (this curious street name 'humpback cat road' was inherited from an old tanner's sign).

## RUE DES CHATS BOSSUS

### Ragot
**1 rue des Chats Bossus**
This is a very large (200 sq.m)

exhibition style shop. On sale are some beautiful items for the home such as crystals, procelains, sculptures etc.

### Sonia Rykiel
**9 rue des Chats Bossus**
Own label designs can be purchased in this a huge boutique. All sizes catered for.

### Deschilder
**6 rue des Chats Bossus**
This type of shop is called a  'maroquinerie' in French which loosely translates into 'a boutique selling fancy leather goods'. Take a look inside and you will find lots of fancy leather creations by Yves St Laurent, Calvin Klein, Kenzo, Sonia Rykiel, Cartier and Moschino. All the names are here.

### Michel Ruc
**23-25 rue des Chats Bossous**
**Tel: 03 20 15 96 16**

Don't be fooled by the antiquated look of the façade. Inside there are the latest looks from Gaultier, Boss and Armani

From here turn right **rue des Arts** and right again into **rue des Clefs**

### Rouge
**15 rue de la Clef**
**Tel: 03 20 74 19 20**
Rouge offers a selection of hip attire where new designers get to try out their labels to an audience of young shoppers. In the meantime heavyweights like DKNY keep the clientelle coming in.

### IEO
**33 rue de la Clef**
**Tel: 03 02 01 65 26**
This is an unusal shop which brings Indian clothing scarves, jewlels and 90 types of natural incense to France.

Alternatively, **Antique lovers** should walk in the opposite direction into **rue Basse.**

## RUE BASSE

### Antique Shop
**16 rue Basse**
**Tel: 03 20 51 52 97**
This simply named Antique shop sells all sorts of lovely antique furniture, plates, trinkets and lights in a very pretty, market style environment.

### Antiquite Aladin
**26 rue Basse**
**Tel: 03 20 06 61 94**
It is attractively laid out with statues, vases, lights amid other interesting objects.

### Bleu Natier
**26 rue Basse**
Though not selling antiques, they do have a fine collection of furniture designed in the spirit of the 30's, 40's and 50's.

### Covent Garden
**52 rue Basse**
**Tel: 03 28 36 42 73**
This shop should be called 'Cat Garden'. The woman who owns the shop is nothing less than a cat freak. Every item in the shop either is a cat or has a cat motif. There are bronze cats, ceramic cats, paper mâché cats, post cards, pictures and cat cartoons.

Turn right into **rue Esquermoise** and right again into **rue Jean-Jacques Rousseau.**

## RUE JEAN-JACQUES ROUSSEAU

### N de B Haute Mode
**6 rue Jean-Jacques Rousseau**
Regulars at Ascot wishing to augment their hat collection should visit this hat shop. Here hats are created by the award winning hat designer Nathalie Sarazin. You can have your hat made to measure.

## RUE ESQUEMOISE

Retrace your steps by turning left into **rue Esquermoise** which you will find adorned with famous names such as **Cartier** and **Gucci** who need no introduction.

### Comtesse du Barry
**21 rue Esquermoise**
**Tel: 03 20 54 00 43**
Delicious delicacies are on sale here. There is a mix of preserved or fresh products from farmyards mainly around South West France but produce from the rest of France is also on sale. Temptations include Foie gras, smoked salmon, terrines and some beautifully gift wrapped savoury items ideal as giving as souvenir presents.

### Clergerie
**24 rue Esquermoise**
This is a fabulous high fashion clothes shop with high prices.

The clothes are frequently recommended in Elle magazine and the designer wear is always one season ahead. So even if you buy clothes in the sale, you are in fact buying trendy clothes.

### Accessoir'In
**25 rue Esquermoise**
This outlet is best described as a designer version of Accessorize. Alongside the unusual collection of jewellry is a collection of gloves, bags, scarves and hats in the up-to-the-minute designs of Christian Lacroix, Yves Saint-Laurent, Kenzo Charles, Jourdan and Karl Lagerfeld.

### Marlboro Classics
**26 rue Esquermoise**
You don't have to be a smoker to shop here. Ironically, the ensemble of well-designed sportswear and walking gear all talks of healthy lungs and fitness.

### La Compagnie Des Marques
**26 rue Esquermoise**
For those of you who do not wish to spend all you shopping budget on expensive clothes this outlet may prove a more sensible option. This outlet operates much like a factory shop. There is a daily delivery of branded clothes at reduced prices and with a little digging, you can uncover some really good bargains.

### Maison de Campagne
**75 rue Esquermoise**
**Tel: 03 20 31 15 30**
Lille is full of interior design shops, a testament to how full of young married there are in the city. This outlet has a truly stylish range of furniture, cooker items or ornaments to add a dash of country cottage to your home.

### Roche Bobois
**76 rue Esquermoise**
Roche Bobois is home to some absolutely beautiful and original classic French furniture and a variety of room accessories. They do have an outlet in London on the Finchley Road, but the collection is not the same. They believe that French tastes in furniture differ. If you do decide to buy anything here, they will deliver.

Walking the length of **rue Esquermoise** will bring you to the main road, **rue National**. However before you reach the take a left turn into **Rue du Cure St Etienne** and a right into **rue Lepelletier**.

## RUE LEPELLETIER

### Cafe Coton
**20 rue Lepelletier**
**Tel: 03 20 55 22 32**
This shop is dedicated to 100% cotton shirts displayed in order of colour for easy reference.

**Dress Code**
**25 rue Lepelletier**
**Tel: 03 20 13 85 93**
This shop offers men top quality designer clothes and accessories. The Stéphane Plassier underwear is truly exclusive as they are only sold in Lille.

**Insolence**
**34 rue Lepelletier**
**Tel: 03 20 06 92 04**
This is one of the top outlets for lingerie that is all at once both chic and sexy. The designs of Marlies Dekkers are on sale, but you will have to dig deep. But what price do you put on sexiness?

Follow the road round to the right into **rue de la Bourse**, cross over **rue Esquermoise** to **rue National**.

**RUE NATIONAL**

**Printemps**
**41-45 rue Nationale**

---

**CHOCOLATE PASSION CLUB**

Lille has its very own 'Chocolat Passion Club' situated right in the heart of Lille run by the confisserie Trogneux Chocolatier.

Their aim is to advise and share their knowledge with a 'demanding and well-informed' consumer as well as to provide their chocolate in tip top condition.

Trogneux
Chocolatier
67 rue
Nationale
59800 Lille
Tel: 03 20 54 74 2
Closed Sun and Mon am.

Why not try:

Le Noir de Houlle
Black chocolate with the local genièvre de Houlle

**Tel:03 20 63 62 00**
This is Lille's most famous department store, a branch of the famous Parisian store - think Debenhams.

### Maison du Porte-Plume
**78 rue National**
If you are looking for a present for someone who has enough ties or perfumes already, you could choose a pen.
At La Maison de Porte-Plume (the house of the quill) there a large range of pens catering for all tastes from gaudy to trendy to very elegant with a price range to match.

Make your way into the **Grand Place.**

GRAND PLACE

### L'Homme Moderne,
**Galerie Grand-Place**
Presents should be fun. On sale there are ultra modern gadgets and items which are not essential but are fun to have anyway.

Walk across the square into **rue Neuve**.

RUE NEUVE

### Amphitrite
**3 rue Neuve**
**Tel: 03 20 54 93 88**
Jewellery is a highly personal matter of choice. This outlet offers a truly original collection of Réminiscence, Clio Bleue and Nereides jewels. Items made from ebony wood are truly beautiful.

Turn left into **rue de Béthune**.

RUE BÉTHUNE

### Benjamin
**45 rue de Béthune**
**Tel: 03 20 54 69 67**
Benjamin has been providing the finish touches of the best dressed since 1926. You will

## Bargain Hunting

Believe it or not, amid the glamour and speciality shops, there is also a bargain shop worth pointing out. So this is for those of you not worried about designer labels.

### Tati
12-15 rue Faidherbe
Tel: 03 2 74 00 00
Amazingly sweaters go for a couple of euros, clothes and jewellery at stupid prices and wedding dresses that cost the same as a quality meal in a restaurant. If you can be bothered to pan through the dross, you'll find some really good golden buys. Kylie Minogue once wore an outfit that was inspired by Tati's own-label pink gingham. The artist Hockney was also inspired to paint the pattern and the locals know they are on to a good thing here.

find a pretty shop specialising in all types of hats, scarves, gloves and even brollies.

### San Diego
**57 rue de Béthune**
This speciality shop which will spur delight in those with cowboy tastes. On sale are authentic Mexican boots, Montanas made of shark, belts, bomber jackets, lighters, watches, Doc Martens, python boots and other accessories to help complete the picture.

### La Carterie
**57 rue de Bethune**
Still stuck for a present? This is an eccentric shop selling the kind of gifts you can only give to someone who can giggle when presented with a loo shaped ashtray.

Retrace your steps and before your reach **rue Neuve**, turn left into **rue de la Vieille Comédie**.

# Shopping - What's in Store

## RUE DE LA VIEILLE COMEDIE

**Le Comptoir des Cotonniers**
**1 rue de la Vieille Comédie**
**Tel: 03 20 15 17 30**
Quality clothes for women sold in a very pleasant environment at reasonable prices.

**Parabot**
**8 rue de la Vieille Comédie**
**Tel: 03 02 54 67 78**
Ask for shoes, and you will be told that they only sell Parabots. Certainly they are footwear, but they are sturdy as well as elegant.  The high prices are justified by the quality of the shoes, er sorry.... parabots.

Make your way back to **rue de Béthune** and cross over the cross roads with **rue Neuve** into **rue du sec Arembault** and turn left into **rue de Paris**.

## RUE DE PARIS

**Jadi'Press**
**24 rue de paris**
**Tel: 03 02 13 04 06**
Postcards, newspapers and cassets galore dating back to 1880. You could come away with a newspaper printed on your date of birth.

Turn right into **rue des Ponts de Comines** and **left into Rue Faidherbe**.

## RUE FAIDHERBE

**Mad Man**
**6 rue Faidherbe**
**Tel: 03 20 31 10 32**
This is a pile 'em high sell 'em cheap outlet where by rummaging through the designer menswear labels you can find a Pierre Cardin or YSL shirt at up to half the original price. Must be worth a punt.

*Euralille epitomises everything we
have come to expect from an
indoor shopping complex.
A huge choice of chain stores, and restaurants -
and cover from the rain.*

Since 1993 a whole new ultra modern urban district has emerged just 100 yards away from the old town. It is not quaint or particularly charming yet it is the hub and the reason for Lille's newly found stardom - Eurallille.

The area comprises two important train stations, **Lille-Flandres** and the newer **Lille-Europe**. Situated between the two stations is the Euralille

shopping complex. Eurostar passengers will be met with its huge glass frontage immediately as they step out of the huge glass fronted station.

The Centre Euralille indoor shopping complex was designed by the French architect Jean Nouvel in a highly futuristic style. The sheer modernity of the design offers a stark contrast to the quaint shopping areas just a few minutes walk away. As well as the immense Carrefour hypermarket (tel: 03 20 15 56 00), the complex contains over 140 shops lining spacious walkways over a massive 90,000 square metres. Shopping includes a variety of French chain stores for men, women and children as well as sports gear, household goods, music and computer products. Here's a selection:

## Artès
**Euralille**
**Tel: 03 20 78 06 51**
Gifts galore inspired, as the name of the outlet suggests, by the works of great artists.

## Loisirs et Créations
**Euralille**
**Tel: 03 20 51 39 01**
Creative types, even beginners will find everything they need to pursue their chosen hobby whether it is painting, tie-dying, cross-stitching or ceramics, wood work or art with glass.

## Nature et Découverte
**Euralille**
**Tel: 03 20 78 01 00**
Pamper yourself with the products on sale here knowing that you are doing so in an eco-friendly way.

## Kitchenette
**Euralille**
**Tel: 03 20 55 26 79**
Cheerful kitchenware is on sale here for everyday use.

## Orcana
**Euralille**
**Tel: 03 20 55 23 36**
Orcana sell pretty and sexy lingerie to inspire a little romance.

## Sephora
**Euralille**
**Tel: 03 20 14 99 50**
A mix of scents and aromas gently assault you as you enter Sephora. On display is an impressive range of perfumes, beauty creams and make-up.

*Would you like to buy your clothes at factory prices; or better still, designer clothes at 30-50% off the retail price? Then a trip to Roubaix is in order.*

Historically, Roubaix has always been an industrial town with a long and sometimes, turbulent tradition in the wool and textile industries.

Specialising first in wool, in the latter half of the 1700s, Roubaix was given a charter allowing it the same privileges as Lille to manufacture English textiles. At that time the English were very much at the forefront of textile technology and manufacture, and many English inventions and ideas were incorporated into the manufacturing processes within the factories of Lille and Roubaix.

TOURIST OFFICE
rue de la Tuilerie
Tel: 03 20 65 31 90
Open Mon-Fri 09.00-18.00
Sat 0.900-noon

It was quite a setback when the French Revolution started and unfortunate for the French industry on two counts. First it effectively cut off their access to Britain and therefore the state-of-the-art British technology. Secondly while the French were suffering a political revolution, the British were the driving force behind a highly successful industrial revolution leaving the French way behind.

In 1815, Napoleon was finally defeated in Waterloo and it was business as usual for the textile industry. This new development made the town of Roubaix extremely prosperous. Unfortunately, during 20th century the undulating fortunes of the industry were particularly hard on Roubaix, following a pattern of boom and doom and then severe gloom. In an effort to restore the fortunes of the area, the government has installed certain tax incentives to entice the textile industry back into Roubaix.   The initiative has been very successful in attracting factories, factory shops and mail order companies thereby allowing Roubaix to emerge once again as one of the most important manufacturing centres of France in the textile industry.

There are two really good factory shopping 'cities' to visit in the area.

The original factory shopping centre is called **A l'Usine** and is aptly housed in a former factory. It is a huge complex with a wide selection of 74 chain store factory outlets including those of the mail order companies La Redoute and Les Troise Suisses as well as Timberland, Wrangler, Levi

---

**McArthurGlen**
Designer Outlet Centre
44 Mail de Lannoy
59100 Roubaix
Tel: 03 28 33 36 00
Open Mon-Friday 10am-7pm
Sat  9.30am to 7pm

**By  road.** Take the A22 motorway  (direction of Gand). Exit at junction 11 (N356) then take junction 10 following signs to Centre Ville then Boutiques de Fabricants.

**Train:** From Lille town centre embark at Rihour station, the closest to the Grand Place. take Line 1 direction "4 Cantons". Change at "Gare Lille Flandre" (the next station) take line 2 to Tourcoing - CH Dron", station "Eurotéléport".

**Metro**: Line 2, direction C.H. Dron, Eurotéléport stop.

**Tram:** Direction Roubaix, Eurotéléport terminus

A L'Usine
228 Alfred-Motte, Roubaix
Tel: 03 20 83 16 20
Open Mon-Sat 10am-7pm

**By road**. Take the A22 motorway  (direction of Gand). Exit at Roubaix then Roubaix est. Then take l'Avenue Alfred Motte.

and a host of French designer factory outlets. Though the surroundings are not very glamourous, it seems very popular with the inhabitants of northern France many of whom regularly shop here for their clothes, shoes and furniture on a regular basis.

The **MacArthurGlen** centre, on the other hand, is an impressive collection of mainly French designer factory outlets. As you would expect, the complex is based in very attractive grounds - just above the Euroteleport transport hub - where designer brands have set up shop to sell off excess and end-of season merchandise. The discounts are between 30-70% off retail prices and when the sales are on the prices are very tempting.

The centre has 50 or so outlets housing a range of famous French fashions and accessories for the kids, men and women. Names include Adidas, Samsonite, Carbone, Cacharel, Well-Gossard and Tony Enzo and Disney's designer label Donaldson.

---

CHEZ RITA

49 rue Daubenton, Roubaix Tel: 03 20 26 22 882 Open Mon-Fri 12 to 14.00
While in Roubaix take time out from shopping to visit Chez Rita. Once a waffle factory, but now the sprawling building is used by young artists. Every inch is a working studio and for a small fee you can roam among them, tour the studio and enjoy the art-deco engraved glass. There is a café on site where salads, country paté and locally brewed ale is served.

*No wine is grown in this part of France but the fiery local tipple is Genièvre - an acquired taste!*

Lille is situated in the heart of a region without vines but blessed with a fertile land ideal for growing hops and cereals for beer and also for producing the drink so fondly known as 'l'eau de vie' (water of life) - Genièvre.

> **Emile Zola would order a 'bistouille' or a 'g'nieff' of gin to accompany his coffee**

Genièvre or Genever in Dutch, means juniper and as the juniper berry is the principal ingredient, the berry has given its name to this highly aromatic and distinctive style of gin.

As a spirit, gin is extremely refined due to the numerous distillation processes it has to undergo. As a result it contains no hangover inducing higher alcohols, despite having an alcoholic content of 49%.

For this reason it has always been known as 'the purest of all spirits'.

Nevertheless its purity certainly did not elevate its public perception in the past and for a long time it was regarded a rather working-class tipple. But fashions change and these days it is very highly regarded.

Up until the end of the 17th century Genièvre had always been imported into France from Holland. By the eighteenth century production of the spirit began in earnest in Northern France.

The exact nature of the recipe tends to be a closely guarded secret by all three of the distilleries in Houlle, near to St Omer, Wambrechies (known at the genièvre gin town which became a European classified heritage site) and in Loos near to Lille each producing gin with subtle differences. You can however, expect wheat, malt and oats and juniper.

Though a meal is generally washed down with beer, traditionally it should be finished off with a glass of Genièvre.

---

**How to drink a bistouille or g'nieff**

**Method One**
Down the gin first and follow soon after with the coffee.

**Method Two**
Add a nip of gin and mix well with the coffee before drinking.

---

**THE DISTILLERIES**

**Genièvre Clayssens**
16 rue de la Distillerie
59118 Wambrechies
Tel: 03 20 14 91 91
This distillery has been around since 1817 and still uses the original wooden machinery. The distillery and shop are open throughout the year for tasting and sales. Both groups and the general public are welcome and a tour ends with a generous tasting session.

**Distillerie Persyn**
62910 Houlle
Tel: 03 21 93 01 71
The distillery is geared up for groups only.

**Distillerie de Loos**
30 rue Gambetta
BP98 59120
Loos
Tel: 03 21 07 10 77
The distillery welcomes groups of between 30 to 60 people. As well as tastings and sales, there is also a museum.

*In 1890 there were 500 breweries in Nord Pas-de-Calais. By 1985 there were just six. But things are looking up...*

The Nord-Pas-de-Calais is an area where the beer brewing industry has experienced both the heady high of boom times and sharply contrasting lows. Where there were once over 500 breweries, there were just 6 by 1985.

Nevertheless the region has always been considered a major brewing and beer-drinking area. In fact, in recent years there has been a renaissance in micro brewing in the region and this is reflected in the interest in beer shown by the people and in particular the student population of Lille. Lille is fast becoming the French capital of beer.

Most beer production is in two major French regions: Strasbourg to the East and in French Flanders in the North. The latter can be tracked from Dunkerque through Lille and then to the deeply rural regions of Hainaut and Avesnois. Some of the breweries belong to the hop growers.

One of these worth visiting is a working farm near the tiny village of Bailleul :

**Ferme-Brasserie Beck.
Eeckelstraete, 59270 Bailleul
Tel 03 2849 03 90.**
It is owned by the Beck family and has been in Beck ownership for generations. The men it seems marry in the labour. They produce their own dairy products, cereals, raise and breed horses and other farm animals.

The beer they produce is a fine example called

**Hommelpap** (Flemish for hops) and has a hefty 7% abv. Its bitterness differentiates it from other Flemish beers since many Flanders beers are rich and sweet.

*'Drinkers here sometimes confuse bitterness with tartness or acidity'* Denis Beck explained *"As a hopgrower, if I was to produce a sweet beer, I'd have difficulty explaining myself."*

A visit and overnight stay is possible as there is a gîte on site. Their delicious beer can be enjoyed with a simple dinner during March and September. Booking in advance is advisable.

Another brewery that welcomes visitors is:
**Brasserie Thiriez, 22 rue de Wormhout, 59470 Esquelbecq.**
**Tel 03 28 62 88 44**
The owner, Daniel Thieriez once worked for Auchan hypermarket in the Lille area before he *"decided to change*

*everything except my wife and do something for which I had a passion".*
He studied brewing in Brussels and now brews two main beers. The first is **La Blonde d'Esquelbecq**, 6.5% abv, a lusciously smooth, yet dry beer. The other is **l'Ambrée d'Esquelbecq**, which is sweeter and spicier on the palate due to the orange peel and liquorice additives.

It seems that the beer **Germinal** has some glamorous connections. When Claude Berri produced a film in 1993 based on Zola's novel 'Germinal' - a story about conflicts between miners and pit owners. He and his actors, including singer Renaud and Gérard Depardieu were appalled at the level of economic depression in the area. In an effort to alleviate the problems, some of the film's profits were used to fund a charitable association called 'L'Association Germinal' to help local businesses. In this vein a brewery was in the mix of newly created businesses. The beer is produced by **Brasserie des Amis Réunis** in **St Amand des Eaux**, in a former abattoir. The owners, as the name suggest, are three long time friends. Germinal Blonde and the fruity Ambrée are both a little spicy and both 6.5% abv and are widely available in northern France.

Another widely available beer is the amusingly named Bière des Sans Culottes (7.5%abv) (beer without trousers, a term referring to the pantalon-wearing revolutionaries to distinguish themselves from the culotte-wearing ruling classes in 1789). The beer is brewed by **La Choulette, 16 rue des Ecoles, Hordain**

**Tel: 03 27 35 72 44**
This brewery has been at the forefront of the revival of bière de garde in Northern France and remains true to the tradition of brewing its beer in copper boilers. Other beers in their range are the 7.5% perfumed, sweetish Blonde Choulette and the golden coloured, fragrant, caramel style Ambrée Choulette.

**The Brasserie Castelain, 13 rue Pasteur, 62410 Bénifontaine, Wingles Tel: 0033 (0)321 08 68 68**
known most notably for its Ch'ti range of beers was founded in 1926 by the Delomel family. Today it is still a family run business and is one of the most progressive French breweries with highly successful marketing. Their beers are available everywhere in France and the UK too. The Ch'ti Blonde is sweet and fruity with a touch of spice and the Ch'ti Brune hints at liquorice with roasted malt. Both have a 6.4% abv. The dark brown Ch'ti Triple

(7.4%) is bottom fermented with a bitter hop character and notes of citrus fruit.

Ch'ti is also the nickname for people from the North of France because they use the 'ch' sound so liberally. More recently it refers to their 'bon vivant' nature.

Lille is home to **Bars de France**, a company who in 1986 started a brew-pub business. The term brew-pub refers to an establishment that brews its own beer and also has a kitchen so food is available too. Their business is propagated on a franchise basis and so all branches are similar in their wood decor. The first pub was opened in Lille in 1986 called **Les 3 Brasseurs, 22 place de la Gare, Lille, opposite the station. Tel 03 20 06 46 25**

The beers brewed at each outlet have the same recipe. Their Blanche de Lille (4.6%)

is sweetly fragrant with hints of citrus fruit. Other beers served are Ambrée (6.2%) Blonde (4.6%) and Brune (6.3%) all tend towards being dry.

**Brasserie Duyck**
**113 Route Nationale, Jenlain**
**Tel 03 27 49 70 03**
produces Jenlain, (6.5%) the dark amber easy drinking beer that for some time during the 1970s had the good fortune of developing a cult status amongst the student population of Lille. This popularity enabled the brewery to finally expand.

Some of the beers of **Le Brasseurs de Gayant** are somewhat adventurous. Beers such as La Goudale (7.2%) is obviously hoppy, with sharp, strong wheat flavours on the palate. Another example of something a little different is Bière du Demon at 12% alcohol - a beer named after the devil - is the second strongest pale beer in the world.

The accolade for the strongest beer in the world goes to the golden coloured, top fermented Belzebuth with a massive 15% abv. The brewery responsible is located in Ronchin, a suburb of Lille. **Brasserie Jeanne D'Arc 38 rue Anatole, Ronchin Tel 03 20 16 92 92** Visitors are welcome, and tours are laid on at around 6 euros a head. They also brew the widely available Alsatia range.

There are major French breweries too such as **Kronenbourg/ Kanterbrau** who produce the world famous 1664 (6.9%) and the low alcohol beer, Koenigsbier (2.6%) as well as Mutzig and Pelforth. The latter is situated near Lille and owned by **Heineken, rue du Houblon, ZI de la Pilaterie, 59370 Mons-en-Baroeul Tel 03 20 33 67 56**

They produce light and dark lagers such as the popular Pelforth Blonde (5.8%) and Pelforth Brune (5.2% & 6.5%) all widely available in France.

Probably the highest selling beer of Northern France is St-Omer Blonde de Luxe (4.6%) brewed by: **Brasserie de St-Omer 9 rue Douard Devaux, 62500 St.Omer Tel: 0321 98 58 20**.

Their brews tend to be made in the popular, French lager style 'bière blonde'and are cheap to buy. Any warehouse or supermarket will sell it.

Many Flemish dishes are cooked with beer and the most popular beer to use is the locally brewed, very full bodied and flavoursome 3 Monts (8.5%). It is produced by **Brasserie de St-Sylvestre** in **Steenvoorde**, and you can taste it in many a 'flamiche' - cheese tart.

***Lille offers an eclectic mix of Flemish, French and international cuisine.***

You can find almost all types of national and international cooking in French Flanders and especially in the very cosmopolitan Lille. Not that France itself does not contribute heftily to the well-being of the taste bud. Indeed, French culinary diversity is very much inspired by France's variety of landscape and locally farmed produce and Lille is no exception.

Typically Flemish food can be tasted in an 'estaminet' - a bistro style bar/restaurant - found only in Flanders.

### FLEMISH CUISINE

What a shame it would be to miss out on typically Flemish dishes that make the cuisine of French Flanders so unique. If you see dishes on the menu with names that are almost impossible to pronounce, such as Pot'je vleesch or Flamiche aux Zermezeelois, you can be sure that these are of Flemish origin.

Ingredients such as prunes, raisins, brown sugar, chicory and beer (especially Bière des Trois Monts) find their way into much of the Flemish cooking.

The cuisine actually includes soup à la bière - beer soup, Pâté à la Bière - beer paté, and beer flavoured ice-cream. Unsurprisingly, Flemish beer is also one of the area's most popular liquid refreshments. When the meal is over, traditionally, it will be completed with a glass of genever or coffee spiced with a little chicory.

The cheeses served tend to be local cheeses with powerful flavours such as Maroilles.

Flamiche au Maroilles, a creamy very flavoursome quiche, is probably the most famous cheese dish of Northern France. Many a cheese tart is made with it, served both hot and cold. One example is the flamkuche. This has a crusty base topped with melted cheese, as well as onions and *lardons* - small pieces of ham. When it has been served, roll it up and eat it with your fingers. Ideally, it should be washed down with a glass of Belgian or French beer.

Most restaurants will offer Flemish dishes, distinguishable by their tongue twisting names.

Some still have chitterling sausages, beef or chicken bouillon, rabbit with raisins, prunes or mustard, pigeon, black pudding, pigs trotters,

sorrel soup, pumpkin soup or even fat-bacon soup included on their menus.

For authenticity though, it is worth seeking out an estaminet the Walloon word for café. When you enter an estaminet and you eye the old world décor, simple dark wood furniture, ceilings and walls enlivened with dried hops, antique pots, pans and old musical instruments you know you are witnessing a snapshot of a bygone Flemish age.

At an estaminet you can enjoy typically Flemish food served in a typically Flemish decor and in a very relaxed atmosphere.

There are no expectations. You can enjoy a beer or two, or perhaps a meal and if you run out of conversation, feel free to pick up one of the old traditional Flemish board games lying around, such as 'billard Nicolas' and 'grenouilles' to help pass the time.

*If you are on a gastronomic adventure and want to take your taste buds on a Flemish journey then here are some typically Flemish dishes to try:*

### Andouille
A big pork, chitterling and tripe sausage. Served cold.

### Andouillette
This is a pork, chitterling and tripe sausage which is grilled and served hot. This dish originates from Arras and Cambrai areas.

### Anguille Au Vert
Sauteed eel cooked in green herbs, spinach, sorrel and wine sauce. It is served on fried bread.

### Boudin Blanc
A white pudding style sausage poached in a sauce or wine.

### Boudin Noir
Black pudding.

### Carpe à la bière
Local carp is cooked with butter and onions, shallots, celery, bay and thyme and baked with a local beer and spiced bread.

### Coq à la Bière
This chicken stew is cooked in beer and juniper gin and prepared with mushrooms.

### Carbonnade à la Flamande
A popular beef stew dish based on thinly sliced beef, slow-cooked for three hours in beer and onion then sweetened with brown sugar.

### Carquelots
Smoked herrings - a speciality of Dunkerque.

### Faisan à la Flamande
Pheasant cooked in beer.

Planche de Lard Fermier

## Flamiche
This is the Flemish word for cake and can be sweet or savoury. The best known is made with leeks, and sometimes Maroilles cheese.

## Gaufres à la citrouille
A deep fried pumpkin waffle then cooked with vegetables and rum.

## La Goyère au Carré de Vinage
A very rich cheese pie served hot.

## Hochepot
This is a filling stew Flemish style. A mixture of beef, lamb, veal, pork, pigs ears and tails, with cabbage and root vegetables, herbs and spices. The word hochepot is an old French word meaning "to shake".

## Lapin au Pruneaux
Rabbit cooked with prunes. This dish has its origins in Poland but is widely embraced as a typically Flemish dish.

Langue Lucullus

This dish is a mix of foie gras (ducks liver) and smoked tongue.

Pigeonneau

Pigeon is often found on Flemish menus.The pictured dish is called 'Pigeonneau au pain d'épices entier et décarcassé - whole pigeons in ginger bread. (prepared by Aupres de mon Arbre, just outside Cassel).

Planche

This describes a wooden board upon which you get a selection of items. This could be a platter of different pâtés, cheeses, or meats or a variety of all these. You can also get a planche of beers or fruit juices.

Potjevleesch

Probably the most popular Flemish dish, potjevleesch originates from Dunkerque and comprises a terrin of three meats, veal,pork and rabbit or chicken, duck and rabbit.  The meat is cooked with onions, garlic and white wine, lemon and tomatoes and served in a golden jelly.  It is eaten cold and sometimes served with fries or just a salad.

Pigeonneau
Aupres de monm Arbres
Cassel

Potjevleisch as served at
Estaminet T Katseel Hof
8 rue St Nicolas, Cassel

# Eating Out - A Menu Guide

Tarte au Fromage

Le Poulet au Maroilles
A pungent dish comprising chicken cooked in the strong Maroilles cheese.

Smakeluk
Rabbit cooked in beer.

Soupe à l'Ail
This is garlic soup. A speciality of Douai.

Soup à la Bière
Soup made with cream, beer and onions.

Tarte au Fromage
also known as
Flamiche au Zermezeelois
This is a cheese tart - usually made with Maroille cheese -

served warm and generally accompanied with salad or French fries

The word Flamiche is the Flemish word for 'cake' or 'flan'. The most popular flamiche is made with leeks.

Veau Flamande
A sweet tasting dish of Veal cooked with dried apricots, prunes and raisins.

Waterzoi
This refers to a dish of either mixed freshwater fish such as a carp or poultry such as chicken. It is cooked with vegetables and cream and served in a thick spicy sauce.

Note:
Restaurants generally open between 12-2.30pm for lunch and again between 6-10.30pm for dinner.

*There is a large cosmoplitan range of
restaurants in Lille.
Here are some suggestions.*

### Alcide
5 rue des Débris St Etienne
Te: 03 20 12 06 95
Tariff: From £12.00
à la carte £15.00
Cuisine: Regional food is
available in this brasserie cum
restaurant. Last orders 11pm.

### Le Cardinal
84 Façade de L'Esplanade
Tel:  03 20 06 58 58
Tariff: From £14.00
à la carte £25.00
Cuisine: Nouvelle and
traditional gastronomic food.
Last orders 10pm.. Closed
Sunday.

### La Cave aux Fioles
39 rue de Gand
Tel:  03 20 55 18 43
Tariff: From £6.00
à la carte £20.00
Cuisine: Traditional and
regional food in a charming
Old Town setting, Two houses
are linked by an internal
courtyard.

### Claire de Lune
50 rue de Gand
Tel: 03 20 51 46 55
Tariff: from £10
à la carte £18.00
Cuisine: Traditional French
food serived in an intimate
atmosphere. Dishes include
mixed grills and stuffed veal.
On Sundays they serve a
particularly good brunch.
Closed Sat and Tue and 2
weeks in July.

### Aux Deux Moutons
2 bis, ru des Malfonds
Tel: 03 20 42 84 61
Tariff: £5
à la carte £9.00
Cuisine: Charcoal grills and
roast meats are the speciality.
The restaurant is air
conditioned.

**La Champlain**
rue Nicolas Leblanc
Tel: 0320 54 81 52
Tariff: £15.00
Cuisine: A gastronomic
restaurant serving nouvelle
and regional food. The meals
are beautifully prepared and
served in a rambling bourgeois
house. Closed Saturday
afternoon and Sunday
evening.

**La Chicorée**
15 place Rihour
Te:l 03 20 54 81 52
Tariff: A la carte £12
Cuisine: Regional and
traditional food,
This restaurant is ideal for
nocturnals as it is open until
6am.

**La Cloche**
13 place du Théâtre
Te:l 03 20 55 35 34
Tariff: à la carte from £5 to
£10.00
Cuisine: Brasserie style
serving regional specialities.
There is also a wine bar where

you can buy by the glass and
a wine cellar where you can
buy a bottle or two to go.

**A Côte aux Arts**
5 place du Concert
Tel: 03 20 52 34 66
Tariff: A la carte from £15
Cuisine: Regional - menu
includes sardines, stuffed pigs
trotters, chitterling sausages
and steak. Last orders at
11pm. Closed Sunday.

**La Ducasse**
95 , rue Solférino
Lilles Les Halles
Tel: 03 20 57 34 10
Tariff: various
Cuisine: Regional.
A casual restaurant, with a
lively, young atmosphere.
Music is provided by a
mechanical contraption called
a Ducasse. The Flemish menu
is inside a comic book.
Speciality beers are served.

**La Ferme des Hirondelle**
1 rue Léon Gambetta
59273 Fretin
Tel: 03 20 64 79 44

This is an old farm which has been divided into two parts, a pub which serves sandwiches, black puddings and soup, and a theatre in the barn.
Ronny Couteure tells stories and Dianne Vanden Eijnden sings for children.

### Le Flibustier
49/53 rue Léon Gambetta
Tel: 03 20 30 16 16
Tariff: £15
Cuisine: Traditional food in a bar with a disco and karaoke festivities.

### Brasserie Flore
11 place Rihour
Tel: 03 20 57 97 07
Tariff: £10.00
Cuisine: A mix of Flemish and traditional cooking within a convivial air-conditioned atmosphere.

### A l'Huitrière
3 rue des Chats Bossus
Tel: 03 20 55 43 41
Tariff: £30.00
à la carte £38.00
Cuisine: Gastronomic restaurant specialising in fish and seafood. It is regarded as the best fish restaurant in Lille.

### Le Hochepot
6 rue du Nouveau Siècle
Tel: 03 2054 17 59
Tariff: £10.00
à la carte £20.00
Cuisine: Mostly regional food with a dash of panache and large range of beers to wash the dinner down.

### Le Jardin du Cloître
17 quai du wault
Tel:  03 20 30 62 62
Tariff: £10.00
à la carte £25.00
Cuisine: Traditional food, The restaurant is in a fabulous setting under an atrium glass roof. The building was originally a 17th century convent. Dinner is served to piano or harp music. Closes at 10.30pm

### Brasserie de la Paix
25 place Rihour

Tel: 03 20 54 70 41
Tariff: From £10.00
à la carte £20.00
Cuisine: Traditional and seafood.
The restaurant is decorated in 1930s style.

### Les P'tites Cotes
23 Boulevard d J B Lebas
Tel: 03 20 5246 46
Tariff: From £8.00
à la carte menu £10.00
Cuisine: Flemish specialities and grills.
Food served until 10pm, Closed Monday.

### Bella Italia
23/25 rue des Fossés
Tel: 03 20 57 93 33
Tariff:£10.00
à la carte £12.00
Cuisine: Fine Italian cuisine. The restaurant benefits from air-conditioning. Last orders 11.30pm.

### La Terrasse Des Ramparts
Logis de la Porte de Gand

Lille
Tel: 0320 06 74 74
Tariff: From £10.00
à la carte £20.00
Cuisine: Nouvelle and regional food in a 17th century setting,

### Estaminet Trijsel
25 rue de Gand
Tel: 03 20 15 01 59
Tariff: From approx £60
Cuisine: Flemish. Offers celtic background music in an authentic estaminet candle-lit astmosphere. The menu is written in an excercise book. You could start with Les planches dégustation - a wooden tray with various cheeses, patés or beers to taste.Closed Sun and Mon and three weeks in August.

**La Bateau Restaurant**
**Swanny V**
1251 Chemin du Halague
Douai
Tel:   0327 96 39 25
Tariff: From £15.00
Cuisine: Regional and traditional.
The boat sails from Douai or Lille and cruises the canals of the Nord-Pas de Calais.

**A Sébastopol**
12 pl. Sébastopol
Tel:  03 20 40 24 80
Tariff: From £7.00
à la carte £13.00
Cuisine: Speciality cusine from the Nord Pas-de-Calais region is served in a café-brasserie style restaurant. It has a modest dining room but the cooking is very good. The ingredients, we are told, are sourced from local farms. Closed Mon and Tues and for three weeks in August.

For a convivial atmosphere to taste French beers try any of the following in Lille:

**Le Bastringue**,
168 rue de Solférino

**Le Hochepot**
6 rue de Nouveau Siècle

**The Jenlain Café**
43 Rihour

**Taverne du Ch'ti**
253 rue Nationale

An old Flemish eating and drinking establishment called **'Estaminet'** is an ideal place to drink the beer of Northern France. These are found all over Flanders.

Try the only authentic estaminet in Lille

**Estaminet Trijsel**
25 rue de Grande

# Night Life - Cabarets and Spectacles

*Lille has a wealth of nocturnal entertainment from dinner and dance to cabaret extravaganzas!*

### Aux Rêves d'Adam
10 rue de Courtrai
Tel: 03 20 06 04 14
Open Wed +Sat from 8pm
This is a very saucy show with a strip-tease (women strippers) and cabaret with dinner. No wonder it is called 'Adam's Dreams'.

### L'Anaconda
74 boulevard jean-Baptiste-Lebas
Tel: 03 20 88 46 41
Open daily except Saturday and nightly except Sunday. Enjoy Mexican tex-mex food, South American decor, lively salsa dancing and intimate dining. A lovely evening for the energetic.

### L'Autrement Dit
14 rue Royale
Tel: 03 20 51 02 22
There is a pub on the first floor and a vaulted cellar offering different styles of music.

### La Fermette
15 route de Fournes
592320 Erquinghem Le Sec
Tel: 03 20 50 79 80
Open lunchtime and Saturday evening for dinner and dance and Sunday for tea and a dance.The music played here is retro style to attract an audience over the age of 40.

### La Flamme
110 rue Jean Jaurès
59810 Lesquin
Tel: 03 20 87 46 46
Open Sunday pm for a magic show and Saturday evening for dinner and dance to live singers.

### Macumba
Centre Commercial d'Englos
Haubourdin
Tel: 03 20 92 07 44
Open Thurs & Sat 3pm-8pm
A nice way to spend an afternoon if you are into afternoon tea dancing.

**Les Folie's de Paris**
52 avenue du Peuple Belge,
Lille
Tel: 03 20 06 62 64
Tariff:  From £23.50
Open everyday except Sun
evening and Mon.
The show - which changes
every year - has been running
for ten years now. A  fun
evening with dinner and a Las
Vegas style cabaret is on offer.
This fast moving cabaret
spectacle is full of
flamboyance, colourful
sequined and feather
costumes adorning a company

of 20 lively entertainers. Even
though the show is in French,
those with just a smattering of
French can enjoy the evening.
Spoofs of Marily, Piafe Céline
Dion, Gene Kelly, Madonna,
Michael Jackson and even our
Queen are extremely amusing.

Entertainment is thrust upon
you the minute you enter the
door. The outrageously
flamboyant director Claude
Thomas greets each and
every customer.

At the end of the show you are
challenged to spot the real women among the entertainers. As everyone leaves the cast kisses or waves goodbye to each and every member of the audience.

# Night Life - Cabarets and Spectacles

**Petrouchka**
67 rue Royale
Tel: 03 20 31 41 98
Tarif: From £23.00
Open evenings except Sun.
and all day Mon.
The show provides a series of
comedy sketches, so a good
understanding of French is
required. The 'ch'tis' accents of
entertainers Alphone and
Zulma adds to the authenticity
of this regional show.

**Planet Show**
ZA rue du Grand Brut, 51960
Lomme
Tel: 03 20 08 10 50
Tariff:  From £20.00
Open: Tues., Wed. and
Sat.evenings. As well as being
the biggest bowling alley in the
area, this is a restaurant, a bar
with karaoke, and a  floor
show of magicians, comics
and cabaret. A great place to
take the kids.

**La Petite Cave**
2 place Philippe-de-Girard
(rue Nationale)

Tel: 03 20 57 13 34
Tarif: From £20
(some drinks included)
If you like French music then
you will enjoy an evening in
this vaulted wine cellar. Quality
food is accompanied by a
cabaret featuring 100 years of
French music. The show
includes songs by Piaf, Brel,
Celine Dion and Aznavor.

**Les Rois Fainéants**
4 rue de Seclin
Noyelles les Seclin
Tel: 03 20 90 15 90
Tarif: From £20.00
Open Wed and Sat. from
8.30pm and Sun pm
Dinner and dance is on offer,
with magicians, impersonators
and cabaret singers.  The age
group of the clients is between
25-30 years old.

**Magic Country**
4 rue du Bas Chemin, Essars
Tel: 03 21 65 24 83
Tarif: From £20.00
An extraordinary magic show
with dinner.

*The city's population have no shortage
of bars and drinking establishments which
are busy every night*

### Angle-Saxo
36 rue d'Angleterre
Tel: 03 20 51 88 89
Open Mon-Sun 9pm- 2am
An intimate bar serving 100
different types of cocktails and
80 whiskies. Jazz and
classical bands play and there
are accoustic concerts in a
non-smoking atmosphere,

### The Australian Bar
33 place Louise de Bettignies
Tel: 03 20 55 15 15
Open: Daily 5pm-2am
An English speaking Aussie
based bar, with a DJ Tuesday,
Wednesday and Satuday
nights.

### l'L'Ibiza
20 rue Masséna
Tel: 03 20 30 19 50
A fairly new bar playing oldies
from the eighties. A variety of
cocktails are served alongside
various shorts.

### L'Echiquier
Hotel Alliance
17 quai de Wault
Tel: 03 20 30 62 62
Age group 30-60 years
Jazz music via a piano and
bass.

### Jenlain Café
43 place Rihour
Tel: 03 20 15 14 55
Open Wed-Sat 10pm-2am
There's a piano-bar, food is
available and various music is
played.

### Tir Na Nog
30 place philippe Lebon
Tel: 03 20 54 66 69
This is an Irish pub playing
celtic music and out of the 8
draught beers 3 are Irish.

Bars in Lille generally stay
open until 2am. To stay up
later try a night club.

# Night Life - The Discos

*If you feel you can keep up,
dance the night away into the
small hours.*

## Le Latina
42-44 rue Masséna
Tel: 03 20 54 86 70
Open Tues-Sat 8pm-4am
Age group: 20+
Want somewhere with some
Latino spirit? Move your body
to the salsa inside this wood
decorated music bar.

## La Scala
32 pl. L de Bettignies
Tel: 03 20 142 10 60
Age group: 30 +
Open Mon-Sat 10pm-dawn
A very trendy place where you
can dance till dawn to rock,
music from the eighties and
French music. There are two
bars and two dance floors.

## La Macumba
32 pl. L de Bettignies
Tel: 03 20 142 10 60
Age group: 20+
Open Thurs-Sat 10pm-5am
Dance to strobes and neons.

## Opéra Night
84 rue de Trévise
Tel: 03 20 88 37 25
Open Wed-Sat 9pm-5am
Age group: 20-35 years
This is a huge underground
hall with a fabulous reputation
and one of the few located in
Central Lille that is open so
late. Decor is flamboyant with
various statues including
sumo wrestlers, but you can
dance or sit around the bar
with a drink and maybe find
yourself a seat under a sumo.

## L'Amnesia
192 bd V Hugo
Tel: 03 20 30 91 57
Open Wed-Sat 9.30pm-5am
Age group: 20+
Serious dancing goes on in
this charming (as much as a
nightclub can be) disco. When
you feel you can dance no
more you can find relief on
one of the comfortable sofas.

## 'Bon Weekend' is not just a pleasantry - it's a very good deal.

Guests who can stay Friday and Saturday or Saturday and Sunday may benefit for a two nights for the price of one deal at most of the city's hotels. Those using the Bon Weekend deal can also benefit from two-for-the-price-of-one offers on museum passes and the one-hour minis bus tour of the city. To be eligible, stays must be booked eight days in advance. Contact the tourist office on : 03 20 21 94 21 for details.

PLEASE NOTE: All tariffs quoted are in Sterling and are approximate.

### Chez Meaux B&B
104 rue Royale
Tel: 03 20 55 31 32
Tariff:From £20.00 & £35.00
Breakfast: Included in price
A charming bed and breakfast maintained well by the owners. If you are willing to spend a little more you can have the larger of the two suites with a bathroom rather than a suite with a shower. This old town house is located close to Lion d'Or area.

### Best Hotel**
66 rue Littré
Tel: 03 20 54 00 02
Tariff: From £25.00
Breakfast: £3.00
Situated near the Wazemmes market and the Gambetta underground station. Rooms are functional and dining in the restaurant is buffet style.

### Hôtel Brueghel**
5 parvis Saint Maurice
Tel: 03 20 06 06 69
Tariff: From £25.00
Breakfast: £4.00
Situated most discretely opposite the St Maurice church close to the

pedestrianised area. It offers top of the range two star accommodation in 1920s style decor. Antiques are found in the nooks and crannies and wrought iron mirros complete a most pleasant effect.

### Hotel Chagnot**
24 pl. de la Gare
Tel: 03 20 74 11 87
Tariff: From 30.00
its location near the train station means you can dump your luggage and go off explore immediately. Rooms are small but decent..

### De La Paix**
46 bis rue de Paris
Tel: 03 20 54 63 93
Tariff: From 38.00
Breakfast: £5.00
Want to share a room with Matisse or Picasso? The comfortable rooms are decorated with posters of masterpieces of great artists.Conveniently there is a car park nearby.

### De La Treille***
7/9 pl Louise de Bettignies
Tel: 03 20 55 45 56
Tariff:From £40.00
Breakfast: £5.00
This modest hotel has a great location in the heart of the old town, just behind the majestic Notre Dame de la Treille cathedral and near to the Hospice Comtesse ideal for those who spend more time out and about than indoors.

### Grand Hôtel Bellevue***
5 ue Jean Roisin
Tel: 03 20 57 45 64
Tariff: From £80.00
Breakfast: £8.00
It's a good thing that the hotel has double glazing.It overlooks the Grand'Place and this being a young city, night time is remains very noisy till late. However the view of the square is great and it's nice to know Mozart himself stayed here, in the spacious, marbled bathrooms bedrooms.

# Hotels

### Novotel Lille Centre***
116 rue de l'Hlopital Militaire
Tel: 03 28 38 53 53
Tariff: From £80.00
Breakfast: £9.00
You know what to expect from a Novotel. This chain hotel has comfortable rooms with the standard double bed and sofa and writing desk. Its dining room is pleasant enough and the two floor bar is charming and has toys for the kids. Best for families.

### Carlton****
3 rue de Paris
Tel: 03 20 13 33 13
Tariff: From £90.00
Breakfast: £8.50
This four star hotel has four star amenities and has an ideal location on a busy corner in the town centre next to the Chambre de Commerce.

### Alliance Golden Tulip****
17 quai de Wault
Tel: 03 20 30 62 62
Tariff:From £100.00
Breakfast: £10.00
This quality four star hotel located close to the citadel near the canals was once a convent. The charming cloister has been adapted with modern materials such as glass and chrome and gives an unusual effect. Breakfast is a hearty buffet and rooms have all mod. cons.

### Citadines Lille Centre
3 rav Willy Brandt
Tel: 03 20 06 97 82
Tariff: From £35
Breakfast: Cook your own in the kitchenette but buffet breakfasts are £4.50.
For the ultimate in freedom, Citadines offers a great self-catering option. Studios come with kitchenettes, dishwsher, vacuum cleaner and ironing board. Or you can pay for a daily maid. It's location is in the Euralille building and has basement parking.

*It's Dunkirk in English, Dunkerque in French but both are derived from the Flemish term Dune Kerk - The Church of the Dunes*

If you have chosen to start your journey from Dunkerque, you may wish to take a quick look around the area and even stop overnight.

Originally covered by the sea, the site of Dunkerque first made an appearance in 1067. It was just a fishing port then and easily vanquished by the Spanish, French, English and the Dutch.

During the Battle of the Dunes in 1658 it was won by Oliver Cromwell and promptly sold back to the French by Charles II. Dunkerque has remained in French hands ever since.

Unfortunately the fierce and bloody battles of WWII destroyed 80% of Dunkerque. Nevertheless the town has been rebuilt and has both historic and touristic appeal.

**Museum of Fine Arts**
The works displayed include collections from 16-20th centuries and documents tracing the town's history.

**Museum of the Port of Dunkerque**
Originally a tobacco depot, the museum charts the history of the port.

**Shopping**
The best shopping to be had is in Boulevard Alexandre III, Boulevard St Barbe, rue National and rue Clémenceau.

**Markets**
Place du Général de Gaulle market is open Saturday and Wednesday mornings from 8am to 4pm.

**Boat Trips** around the harbour are available.
Tel: 00 33 328 59 11 14

## Restaurants

La Bois de Chêne
48 route de Bergues
Cappelle La Grande
Tel: 03 28 64 21 80
Tariff:£11
Cuisine: Flemish & seafood

L'Estouffade
2 Quai de la Citadelle
Tel: 03 28 63 92 78
Tariff: From £10
Cuisine: Fish specialities

La Fondue
37 rue de Bourgone
Tel: 03 28 63 23 90
Tariff:£7
Cuisine: Fondues

Le Mistral
11 Place Roger Salengro
Tel: 03 28 66 95 38
Tariff: From £7
Cuisine: Traditional and
regional cooking

---

*A good time to be there:*
*25th Feb-4 Mar*
*Dunkerque Carnival*
*Thousands visit the annual*
*carnival. Crowds wearing fancy*
*dress take to the streets*

---

## Hotels
Tariffs are per room

Altea
Tour Reuze
In the town centre.
Tel: 03 28 59 11 11
Tariff: From £28

Le Meunerie****
174 rue des Pierres
Teteghem (just out of
Dunkerque)
Tel: 03 28 68 79 00
Tariff: From £55

Hotel au Rivage**
7 rue de Flandre
Tel: 03 28 63 19 62
Tariff: From £28

Hotel Trianon**
20 rue de la Colline
Tel: 03 28 63 39 15
Tariff: From £
With restaurant

---

**TOURIST OFFICE**
4 place Charles Valentin
Dunkerque
Tel: 00 33 328 66 79 21

# A Detour to Cassel

*"From Cassel you can see five kingdoms: France, Belgium, Holland, England and above the clouds the Kingdom of Heaven".*

*A local saying*

To truly benefit from the Flemish experience a short detour to Cassel deep in the echelons of the Flemish countryside is highly recommended.

Make your way there either on your way to Lille, just fifty minutes from Calais or Dunkerque, or go for an exploratory drive out of Lille, just twenty minutes away.

The historic, typically Flemish town of Cassel is built on a hill, surrounded by the never ending green flat plains of Flanders. Though situated a fair way from the coast - 30km - it still manages to serve as a useful landmark for passing sailors.

The Flemish architecture is the finest in Flanders, and the views are beautiful. Being 176 metres high - the highest point of the area - it seems as though you can see forever, from anywhere in the town.

It was for precisely this reason that **General Foch** made Cassel his headquarters during WWI. From the summit he was able to get an aerial view of the plains and follow the progress of the war. In his honour an equestrian statue of the General stands in the same spot in what is now the public gardens.

Just beyond the statue a little lower down the hill, perches an impressive windmill. The hill was once dotted with over 20 such windmills but numbers have dwindled to just this one.

Though the **Casteel Meulen** is over 200 years old, it still efficiently produces flour. Visitors are welcome to a guided tour and everyone is

given a bag of flour when they leave. The windmill is open from April to September and public holidays.
Tel: 03 28 40 52 55.

Probably the busiest area is the **Grand Place**, the main square. The square, shaped as an oblong, stretches along the hillside close to the Gothic Flemish collégiate church of **Notre-Dame** where Foch often came to pray.

There are a number of other 16-18th century buildings lining the square, one of which is the handsome 16-17th century **Hôtel de la Noble Cour** with a Renaissance doorway framed with grey marble columns. Under the Ancien Régime the Hôtel de la Noble Cour was used as a court room where the local lord would implement justice.

Just off the Grand Place is the **Schoebecque Hotel** where the General stayed. The road was named **rue de Maréchal Foch** after its famous resident.

Around the square there are a few shops and a number of restaurants surrounding the cobbled road, most have a panoramic view to enjoy with your meal.

### Cassel and WW1

Cassel and the surrounding Nord region saw some of the most horrific war scenes, and most ferocious battles during World War I. Hundreds of thousands of young lives were lost for the control and protection of such a small piece of land.

Their cemeteries are poignant in their simplicity - just row after neatly laid out row of small white crosses.
More information about British cemeteries is available from the tourist office:

ARMENTIÈRES TOURIST OFFICE
33 rue de Lille
Armentières
Tel: 03 20 44 18 19
Fax: 03 20 77 48 15

# A Detour to Cassel

Restaurants to try are:

**Estaminet T Katseel Hof**
8 rue Saint Nicolas
Cassel
Opposite the windmill
Cuisine: Typically Flemish
Tariff: From £3.00
Tel: 03 28 40 59 29

**Taverne Flamande**
34 Grand Place
Cassel
Enjoy the views over the flat plains from the rear of this restaurant.
Cuisine: Typically Flemish
Tariff: From FF68
Tel: 03 28 42 42 59

For stylish Flemish cuisine in a romantic setting, a further detour is recommended

**Auberge Auprès de mon arbre**
932 route d'Eecke
Terdeghem
Tarlff: From £8.00
Tel: 03 28 49 79 79
From Cassel take the direction to Steenvoorde. After the main square (small in reality) take first right . Straight ahead to the Inn "Auprès de mon arbre".

---

**Annual Events:**
**Phone first to confirm:**

**Cassel**
5th April
Summer carnival
Tel: 03 28 40 52 55

**Steenvoorde**
16-17th May
Mee-fest
Tel: 03 28 49 77 77

2-3rd October
Hop Festival
Tel: 03 28 49 77 77

**Wormout**
2-4th July
Music Festival
Tel: 03 28 62 81 23

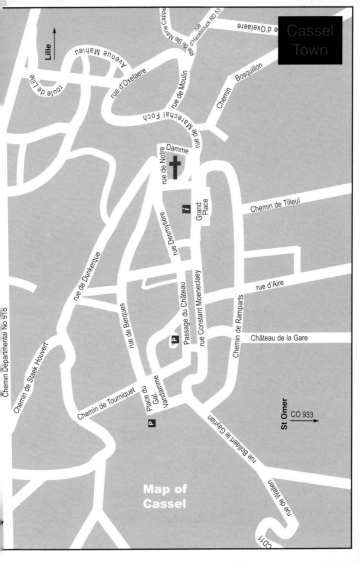

# Practicalities - Driving in France

Driving along the well-maintained roads and motorways in France is a pleasure. But be sure not to break the law.

## En Route:
To comply with French motoring regulations, please note what is and is not essential:

## It is essential:
- To have a full UK driving licence and all motoring documents.
- To be over the age of 18 - even if you have passed your test in the UK.
- Not to exceed 90km/h in the first year after passing your test.
- To display a GB sticker or Euro number plate.
- To carry a red warning triangle.
- To wear rear and front seat belts.
- To affix headlamp diverters. These are widely available in motoring shops or DIY with black masking tape.

## It is not essential:
- To have a green card although very helpful.
- To have yellow headlights.

## Traffic News:
Tune in to Autoroute FM107.7 for French traffic news in English and French.

## Speed Limits
In France speed limits are shown in kilometres per hour **not** miles per hour. Always adhere to these speed limits as in France they are strictly enforced and punishable with a fine or even a ban:

|                  | MPH | km/h |
|------------------|-----|------|
| Toll motorways   | 81  | 130  |
| Dual Carriageways| 69  | 110  |
| Other Roads      | 55  | 90   |
| Towns            | 31  | 50   |

When raining, these speed limits are reduced by 6mph on the roads and 12mph on the motorway. In fog, speed is restricted to 31mph. As well as speed traps, it is useful to know that entrance and exit times through the toll booths can be checked on your toll ticket and may be used as evidence of speeding!

# Practicalities - Driving in France

**Motorways & Roads:**

French motorways (autoroutes) are marked by blue and white A signs. Many motorways are privately owned and outside towns a toll charge (péage) is usually payable and can be expensive. This can be paid by credit card (Visa Card, Eurocard, Mastercard), or euros at automatic gates, so be prepared.

Contact a tourist board for the exact cost. if you have access to the internet click on **www.autoroutes.fr.**

Roads are indicated as:

**A roads -**
Autoroutes - Motorways where a toll is probably payable.

**N Roads -**
 routes nationales - toll free, single lane roads. Slower than A roads.

**D roads -**
Routes départementales - scenic alternatives to A roads.

**C roads -**
routes communales - country roads.

**Breakdown on Motorways:**

If you should break down on the motorway and you do not have breakdown cover,
**DON'T PANIC**, you can still get assistance. There are emergency telephones stationed every mile and a half on the motorway. These are directly linked to the local police station. The police are able to locate you automatically and arrange for an approved repair service to come to your aid.

Naturally there is a cost for this and fees are regulated. Expect to pay around £50 for labour plus parts and around £55 for towing.

An extra 25% supplement is also charged if you break down between 6pm and 8am and any time on Saturdays, Sundays and national holidays.

At the garage, ensure you ask for un Ordre de Réparation (repair quote) which you should sign. This specifies the exact nature of the repairs, how long it will take to repair your vehicle and, importantly, the cost!

# Practicalities - Driving in France

## Roadside Messages:

For safety's sake, it is very important to be aware of the roadside messages:

| | |
|---|---|
| **Carrefour** | Crossroad |
| **Déviation** | Diversion |
| **Priorité à droite** | |
| Give way to traffic on the right | |
| **Péage** | Toll |
| **Ralentir** | Slow down |
| **Vous n'avez pas la priorité** | |
| | Give way |
| **Rappel** | Restriction continues |
| **Sens unique** | One way |
| **Serrez à droite/** | Keep right/ |
| **à gauche** | Keep left |
| **Véhicules lents** | |
| | Slow vehicles |
| **Gravillons** | Loose chippings |
| **Chaussée Déformée** | |
| Uneven road and temporary surface | |
| **Nids de Poules** | Potholes |

## Drink Driving:

French law dictates that a 50g limit of alcohol is allowed - just one glass of wine. Exceed this limit and you risk confiscation of your licence, impounding of the car, a prison sentence or an on-the-spot fine between £20 to £3,000!

## Tyre Pressure:

It is crucial to ensure that your tyres are at the correct pressure to cater for heavy loads. Make sure you do not exceed the car's maximum carrying weight. The following table gives a guide to typical loads:

| | | Weight | |
|---|---|---|---|
| **1 case of** | **Qty** | **kg** | **lbs** |
| Wine | x 2 | 15kg | 33lbs |
| Champagne | x12 | 22kg | 48lbs |
| Beer 25cl | x 2 | 8kg | 18lbs |

## Filling Up:

To fill up, head for petrol stations attached to the hypermarkets as these offer the best value fuel. Petrol stations on the motorway - autoroutes - tend to be more expensive. Though sterling and travellers cheques are not accepted, credit cards usually are. Some petrol stations have automated payment facilities by credit card. These are generally 24 hour petrol stations and tend to be unmanned in the evening but do not rely on them for fuel salvation as they often do not accept international credit cards!

Petrol grades are as follows:

# Practicalities - Driving in France

**Unleaded petrol -**
l'essence sans plomb.
Available in 95 & 98 grades -
equates to UK premium and
super grades respectively.

**Leaded petrol -**
l'essence or Super
Graded as:
90 octane (2 star),
93 octane (3 star)
97 octane (4 star).
Gazole - Diesel Fuel
GPL - LPG (liquefied petroleum
gas)

## IMPORTANT!

☞ IF THERE ARE NO STOP
SIGNS AT THE
INTERSECTION, CARS
MUST YIELD TO THE
RIGHT

☞ CHILDREN UNDER 10
ARE NOT ALLOWED TO
TRAVEL IN THE FRONT

☞ DRIVE ON THE RIGHT,
OVERTAKE ON THE LEFT

## Emergency Phrases:

Please, help
*Aidez-moi s'il vous plaît*

My car has broken down
*Ma voiture est en panne*

I have run out of petrol
*Je suis en panne d'essence*

The engine is overheating
*Le moteur surchauffe*

There is a problem with the
brakes
*Il y a un problème de freins*

I have a flat tyre
*J'ai un pneu crevé*

The battery is flat
*La batterie est vide*

There is a leak in the petrol tank/in
the radiator
*Il y a une fuite dans le
réservoir d'essence/dans le radiateur*

Can you send a mechanic/breakdown
van?
*Pouvez-vous envoyer un
mécanicien/une dépanneuse?*

Can you tow me to a garage?
*Pouvez-vous me
remorquer jusqu'à un garage?*

I have had an accident
*J'ai eu un accident*

The windscreen is shattered
*Le pare-brise est cassé*

Call an ambulance
*Appelez une ambulance*

# Practicalities - Driving in France

## Accidents:

If you do have an accident you must fill out a damage assessment form. Get this from your insurance company before you leave. It must be signed by the other party and in the event of a dispute or a refusal to complete the form you should immediately obtain a constat d'huissier. This is a written report from a bailiff (huisser). In the event of a dispute call the police so that you can make out an official report. If someone is injured call the SAMU (15) or the fire brigade (18). The police are only called out to accidents when someone is injured or a driver is under the influence of alcohol or the accident impedes the flow of traffic.

## Parking:

Illegal parking in France can be penalised by a fine, wheel clamping or vehicle removal. Park wherever you see a white dotted line or if there are no markings at all.

There are also numerous pay and display meters. (horodateurs) where small change is required to buy a ticket. The ticket should be displayed inside the car windscreen on the driver's side.

If you find a blue parking zone (zone bleue), this will be indicated by a blue line on the pavement or road and a blue signpost with a white letter P. If there is a square under the P then you have to display a cardboard disc which has various times on it. They allow up to two and a half hours parking time. The discs are available in supermarkets or petrol stations and are sometimes given away free. Ask for a **disque de stationnement.**

## Services:

On the motorways every

| | |
|---|---|
| 10km | rest areas for short stops |
| 40km | service stations and restaurants |
| 100+km | motels for overnight stops |

## Currency:
The currency used in France is the Euro. This is made up of notes and Euror coins and cents.

When you are looking at a price tag, menu or receive a receipt be aware that unlike the British system of separating pounds and pence with a decimal point, in France there is no decimal point, Euros and cents are separated by a comma.

Unlimited currency may be taken into France but you must declare bank notes of 50,000 Euros or more if you are bringing this back.

## Currency Exchange:
Changing money from sterling to Euros can be expensive. Use your credit card to pay for goods abroad, as credit card companies give a better rate of exchange and do not charge commission when buying goods abroad. Of course you will require some cash. Change your money in the UK where it can be a little more competitive than in France.

In France you can also change money and cash travellers cheques at the post office (PTT), banks, stations and private bureaux de change.

You can also make a purchase in the hypermarkets in Calais in sterling, as change is given in Euros without commission. Though convenient, always be aware of the exchange rate. Some shops do take advantage.

Travellers cheques can be used as cash and if you wish to turn them into cash at a French bank you will receive the face value - no commission.

**Most banks in France do not accept Eurocheques**

## Credit Cards:
Credit cards are widely accepted To use your credit card ensure that you have your passport handy as you may be expected to produce it.

If your card has been rejected in a shop or restaurant, it could be that their card reading machine does not recognise it -

# Practicalities - Money Matters

some French credit cards have a 'puce', a microchip with security information on it. British cards do not. French tourist authorities recommend you say:

Les cartes anglaises ne sont pas des cartes à puce, mais à band magnétique. Ma carte est valable et je vous serais reconnaissant d'en demander la confirmation auprès de votre banque ou de votre centre de traitement.'

which means:
English cards don't have an information chip, but a magnetic band. My card is valid and I would be grateful if you would confirm this with your bank or processing centre.'

If you need to contact:

**Barclaycard**
Tel: +44 (0)1604 234234

**Visa**
Tel: +44 (0)1383 621166

**Visa in France**
Tel: 01 45 67 84 84

**Cashpoints:**
You can use your cashpoint card to get local currency from cash-dispensing machines. This service is available at major banks such as: Crédit Lyonnais, Crédit Agricole and Crédit Mutuel. If the machine bears the same logo as that displayed on your card, such as Visa or Delta, then you can insert your card and follow the instructions. These are likely to be in English as your card will be recognised as British.

Punch in your PIN and press the button marked **Envoi.** When prompted tell the machine how much you want in French francs. You will see phrases such as:

**Tapez votre code secret** -
Enter your pin

**Veuillez patienter** -
Please wait

**Opération en cours** -
Money on its way!

## Shopping:

Shops and supermarkets open and close as follows:

| | |
|---|---|
| Open | 9.00 am |
| Close lunch-time | 12.00 noon |
| Open again | 2.00 pm |
| Close finally | 5.00-7.00 pm |

Most shops are closed on Sunday and some on Monday. Supermarket trolleys (les chariots) require a (refundable) 1 euro piece.

## Taxi!

It is cheaper to hail a taxi in the street or cab ranks indicated by the letter 'T' than order one by telephone. This is because a telephone- requested taxi will charge for the time taken to reach you. Taxi charges are regulated. The meter must show the minimum rate on departure and the total amount (tax included) on arrival.

If the driver agrees that you share the taxi, he has the right to turn the meter back to zero at each stop showing the minimum charge again.

A tip (pourboire) is expected. It is customary to pay 10-15%.

## Public Holidays:

Most French shops will be shut on the following days:

| | | |
|---|---|---|
| Jan 1 | New Year | Jour de l'an |
| Apr* | Easter Monday | Lundi de Pâques |
| May 1 | Labour Day | Fête du Travail |
| May 8 | Victory Day | Armistice1945 |
| May* | Ascension | Ascension |
| May* | Whitsun | Lundi de Pentecôte |
| July 14 | Bastille Day | Fête nationale |
| Aug 15 | Assumption | Assomption |
| Nov 1 | All Saints' | Toussaint |
| Nov 11 | Armistice Day | Armistice 1918 |
| Dec 25 | Christmas | Noël |
| *Dates change each year. | | |

## Tipping:

Tipping is widely accepted in France. However, restaurant menus with the words 'servis compris' indicate that service is included but small change can be left if so desired. The following is the accepted norm for tipping:

| | |
|---|---|
| Restaurants<br>service usually included | Optional |
| Cafés<br>service usually included | Optional |
| Hotels | No |
| Hairdressers | 2 euros |
| Taxis | 2 euros |
| Porters | 2 euros |
| Cloakroom<br>attendants | Small change |
| Toilets | Small change |

# Practicalities - Out and About in France

## Caught on the Hop!
Cafés allow you to use their toilets for free. Shopping centres also have facilities. If you see a white saucer, place a coin or two in it. In the streets you may see the Sanisette, a white cylindrical building. Insert the required coin in the slot to open the door. After use the Sanisette cleans itself.

## No Smoking!
It is forbidden to smoke in public places. However, there are quite often spaces reserved in cafés and restaurants for smokers.

## Pharmacy:
These are recognised by their green cross sign. Staff tend to be highly qualified so are able to give medical advice on minor ailments, provide first aid and prescribe some drugs. Some drugs are only available via a doctor's prescription (ordonnance).

## Doctor:
Any pharmacy will have an address of a doctor. Consultation fees are generally about £15.00.

Ask for a Feuille de Soins (Statement of Treatment) if you are insured.

## Medical Aid:
As members of the EU, the British can get urgent medical treatment in France at reduced costs on production of a form E111 available from the Department of Health and Social Security.

A refund can then be obtained in person or by post from the local Social Security Offices (Caisse Primaire d'Assurance Maladie).

## Electricity:
You will need a continental adapter plug (with round pins). The voltage in France is 220V and 240V in the UK.

## Television/Video Tapes:
French standard TV broadcast system is SECAM whereas in the UK it is PAL. Ordinary video cassettes bought in France will show only in black and white. French video tapes cannot be played on British videos. Ask for VHS PAL system.

# Practicalities - Out and About in France

## Phoning Home:
In France telephone numbers have a 10 digits. To call UK dial the international code 00 44 then the UK number minus the first 0.

To call France from the UK dial the international code 00 33 then the French number minus the first 0.

Phonecards (Télécartes) are widely used and available at travel centres, post offices, tobacconists, newsagents and shops displaying the Télécarte sign. You will need one to use a telephone box. 50 units costs 7.41 euros. 120 units costs 14.74 euros.

Between 8am and 7pm a phone call from France to the UK costs 0.23 euros per minute and 0.12 euros at weekends starting 2pm on Satudays.

Cheap rate (50% extra time) is between 22.30hrs-08.00hrs Monday to Friday, 14.00hrs-08.00hrs Saturday, all day Sunday & public holidays. To call the UK dial 00, at the dialling tone dial 44 followed by the phone number and omit 0 from the STD code.

To call:

| | |
|---|---|
| The operator dial : | 13 |
| Directory Enquiries dial : | 12 |

## Writing Home:
Post offices (PTT) are open Monday to Friday during office hours and half day on Saturday. Smaller branches tend to close between noon and 2pm. Stamps can also be bought from tobacconists. A letter home will cost you 0.46 euros up to 20g.

You can find a post office at the following addresses:

La Poste
Pl. de la République
Tel: 03 20 55 98 32

1 bd Carnot
Tel: 03 20 55 32 52

13-15 rue Nationale
Tel: 03 28 38 18 40

The small but bright yellow post boxes are easy to spot.

# Practicalities - Out and About in France

## What's the Time?

French summer starts on the last Sunday in March at 2am and ends on the last Sunday in October at 3am. Time is based on Central European Time (Greenwich Mean Time + 1 hour in winter and + 2 hours in summer). France is one hour ahead. The clocks are put forward 1 hour in the spring and put back 1 hour in the autumn.

## Passports:

Before travelling to France you need a full 10- year British passport. Non--British nationals require a visa and regulations vary according to your nationality. Contact the French Consulate.

## Pet Passports:

Since 28th February 2000, a scheme has been in force enabling cats and dogs to travel abroad without being subjected to six months quarantine. A blood test is required and a microchip is fitted. Not more than 48 hours before return, the animal must be treated for tics and tapeworms. Only then will it be awarded the official pet passport'. Further information is available from PETS helpline 0870 2411 710.

## Emergency Numbers:

Police     17
Fire       18
Health     15

## Calmette Hospital
Bd du professuer Jules Lelecrc
Tel: 03 20 44 59 62

## Medical Assistance
3 av Louise Michel
Tel: 03 20 29 91 91

## Main Police Station
66bis, bd du Mal Vaillant
Tel: 03 20 62 47 47
Open Mon-Sun 08.00-22.00

## British Embassy
11 square du Dutilleul
Tel: 03 20 12 82 72

## Breakdown Service
205 rue de Paris
Tel: 03 20 52 52 52

## Pound
30 rue F. Combemale
Tel: 03 20 50 90 14

# Practicalities - Conversion Tables

## What's Your Size?
## When buying clothes in France,
## check the conversion tables below
## to find out your size

### Women's Shoes

| GB | | FR | GB | | FR |
|---|---|---|---|---|---|
| 3 | = | 35$\frac{1}{2}$ | 5$\frac{1}{2}$ | = | 39 |
| 3$\frac{1}{2}$ | = | 36 | 6 | = | 39$\frac{1}{2}$ |
| 4 | = | 37 | 6$\frac{1}{2}$ | = | 40 |
| 4$\frac{1}{2}$ | = | 37$\frac{1}{2}$ | 7 | = | 40$\frac{1}{2}$ |
| 5 | = | 38 | 8 | = | 41$\frac{1}{2}$ |

### Women's Dresses/Suits

| GB | | FR | GB | | FR |
|---|---|---|---|---|---|
| 8 | = | 36 | 14 | = | 42 |
| 10 | = | 38 | 16 | = | 44 |
| 12 | = | 40 | 18 | = | 46 |

### Women's Blouses/Sweaters

| GB | | FR | GB | | FR |
|---|---|---|---|---|---|
| 30 | = | 36 | 36 | = | 42 |
| 32 | = | 38 | 38 | = | 44 |
| 34 | = | 40 | 40 | = | 46 |

### Men's Shirts

| GB | | FR | GB | | FR |
|---|---|---|---|---|---|
| 14$\frac{1}{2}$ | = | 37 | 16 | = | 41 |
| 15 | = | 38 | 16$\frac{1}{2}$ | = | 42 |
| 15$\frac{1}{2}$ | = | 39/40 | 17 | = | 43 |

### Men's Suits

| GB | | FR | GB | | FR |
|---|---|---|---|---|---|
| 36 | = | 46 | 42 | = | 52 |
| 38 | = | 48 | 44 | = | 54 |
| 40 | = | 50 | 46 | = | 56 |

### Men's Shoes

| GB | | FR | GB | | FR |
|---|---|---|---|---|---|
| 7 | = | 40 | 10 | = | 43 |
| 8 | = | 41 | 11 | = | 44 |
| 9 | = | 42 | 12 | = | 45 |
| | | | 13 | = | 46 |

### Weights and Measures:

Distance 1.6 km  =  1 mile
Weight 1 kg  =  2.20lbs
Liquid 4.54 litres=  1 gallon
Liquid 1 litre  =  1.76 pints
Length 1m  =  39.37inches
Area 1sq metre  =  1.196 sq yds

### Speed

| kpm | mph | kpm | mph |
|---|---|---|---|
| 50 | 31 | 100 | 62 |
| 70 | 43 | 110 | 68 |
| 80 | 50 | 120 | 75 |
| 90 | 56 | 130 | 81 |

# Practicalities - Custom Guidelines

**In theory there are no limits on the amount of alcohol or tobacco for personal use.
In practice exceeding the Advisory Guidelines, means you could be stopped**

Since 1st January 1993, you are permitted to bring back as much alcohol and tobacco as you like, but it must be for personal use only. So you can happily stock up for Christmas or parties or weddings.

Although H. M. Customs and Excise have no authority to limit the amount you bring back into this country they do have the right to stop you if your purchases exceed the Advisory Guidelines. In this case you may be required to prove that the goods are for your own personal use. That means you cannot buy goods on behalf of anyone else, even your own mother!

If you are stopped, remember that the H.M. Customs officer is looking for bootleggers or those intent on resale. Other products such as mineral water, or any other non-alcoholic or food products, are not limited in any way.

Enjoy.

## Advisory Guidelines
### as set by H.M. Customs & Excise

| | |
|---|---|
| Wine | 90 litres |
| Spirits | 10 litres |
| Fortified wine | 20 litres |
| Beer | 110 litres |
| Cigarettes | 3200 |
| Cigars | 200 |
| Cigarillos | 400 |
| Tobacco | 3 kilogram |

Note: People under 17 are not allowed to bring in tobacco and alcohol